# RECLAIM YOUR LIFE

Essential Guide to Sexual Addiction and Holistic Recovery

Dr Fai Seyed Aghamiri

First published by Ultimate World Publishing 2020
Copyright © 2020 Dr. Fai Seyed Aghamiri

ISBN

Paperback: 978-1-922497-34-5
Ebook: 978-1-922497-35-2

Dr. Fai Seyed Aghamiri has asserted her rights under the Copyright, Designs and Patents Act 1988 to be identified as the author of this work. The information in this book is based on the author's experiences and opinions. The publisher specifically disclaims responsibility for any adverse consequences which may result from use of the information contained herein. Permission to use information has been sought by the author. Any breaches will be rectified in further editions of the book.

All rights reserved. No part of this publication may be reproduced, stored in or introduced into a retrieval system, or transmitted in any form, or by any means (electronic, mechanical, photocopying, recording or otherwise) without the prior written permission of the author. Any person who does any unauthorised act in relation to this publication may be liable to criminal prosecution and civil claims for damages. Enquiries should be made through the publisher.

**Cover design:** Ultimate World Publishing
**Layout and typesetting:** Ultimate World Publishing
**Editor:** Sarah Newton-John
**Cover image:** Lightspring-Shutterstock.com

Ultimate World Publishing
Diamond Creek,
Victoria Australia 3089
www.writeabook.com.au

# Dedication

*I dedicate this book first and foremost to my Lord and Saviour, thanking Him for His sustaining power. I would not have completed this book without His divine intervention and help. This book is also dedicated to the men and women who have been impacted by sex addiction. To the addicts themselves, their partners and families. I have been honoured to get to know you and witness some remarkable transformations. Your courage and stories have been inspiring.*

"He will wipe away every tear from their eyes, and death shall be no more, neither shall there be mourning, nor crying, nor pain anymore, for the former things have passed away."
**Revelation 21:4**

# Contents

| | |
|---|---|
| Dedication | iii |
| Introduction | vii |
| Chapter 1: Definition Of Addiction | 1 |
| Chapter 2: Sex Addiction – An Overview | 5 |
| Chapter 3: The Addict's Circle Of Shame | 9 |
| Chapter 4: Pornography | 11 |
| Chapter 5: Addiction To Masturbation | 23 |
| Chapter 6: Similarities With Other Addictions | 25 |
| Chapter 7: The Brain And Sex Addiction | 29 |
| Chapter 8: Cycles Of Sex Addiction | 33 |
| Chapter 9: Signs Of Sex Addiction | 39 |
| Chapter 10: The Addict's Belief System | 47 |
| Chapter 11: Predatory Flirting And Objectification | 51 |
| Chapter 12: Common Personality Traits | 55 |
| Chapter 13: Connection And Intimacy | 71 |
| Chapter 14: Co-occurring Conditions | 77 |
| Chapter 15: Recovery | 81 |
| Chapter 16: Compassion Vs Condemnation | 101 |

| | |
|---|---|
| Chapter 17: Entering An Intimate Relationship In Recovery | 113 |
| Chapter 18: Real People, Real Stories | 121 |
| Chapter 19: Frequently Asked Questions | 137 |
| About The Author | 143 |
| Acknowledgements | 147 |
| Reference list | 149 |
| Services and Offers | 163 |

# Introduction

This book is about sexual addiction/compulsive sexual behaviours as described by the addicts themselves or impacted family members.

It is intended to be an easy to understand guide for individuals and their loved ones who want to understand sexual addiction and the "why" behind the behaviour.

Additionally, this book is based on current research, available literature, and professional experiences gathered from counselling clients. In order to protect individuals' privacy, pseudo identities and names have been given to certain individuals, and other characters are fully de-identified. The information contained herein is a guide and not intended to be a substitute for professional assessment and treatment.

Dr. Fai Seyed Aghamiri

Both men and women struggle with sexual addiction, women in a smaller percentage compared to men; however, they face the same challenges. This book is intended to give a brief overview and insight into the condition and answer some of the initial "why" questions. Sexual addiction is a multifaceted condition requiring a multifaceted/holistic approach to recovery where the addict and their partners are actively participating in the process.

# CHAPTER 1

# Definition Of Addiction

A revolutionary paradigm shift is occurring in the field of addiction. While "addiction" has historically been associated with the problematic overconsumption of drugs and/or alcohol, the neuroscientific research in this field has changed our understanding over the last few decades. It is now evident that various behaviours which are repeatedly reinforcing the reward, motivation and memory circuitry are all part of the disease of addiction. There are common mechanisms among addictions involving different psychoactive substances such as alcohol, opioids and cocaine; and pathological behaviours such as uncontrolled gambling, internet use, and gaming. Pornography consumption and sexual behaviours have also been similarly described.

Dr. Fai Seyed Aghamiri

## *Behavioural Addiction vs Drug Addiction:*

The basic feature of a behavioural addiction is the failure to resist an impulse, urge, or temptation, and complete an act that is destructive and risky to the individual or to others. According to several studies, the behavioural addictions, such as compulsive sexual behaviours or gambling, are similar to drug use addictions. Individuals with drug addictions, just like individuals with behavioural addictions, report difficulties with impulse control and in resisting the cravings and urges to use drugs.

Due to the growing neuroscientific evidence, in 2011 the American Society of Addiction Medicine (ASAM) formally expanded their definition of addiction to include both behaviours and substances. ASAM considers addiction to be mainly a chronic brain reward disease associated with the brain's circuitry. Notably, impairments in the brain's circuitry can cause social, spiritual, physical and psychological challenges, and can influence the individual to seek relief from discomfort through addictive substances or behaviour. Individuals with drug addiction can commonly face relationship, financial or work-related problems. These problems resemble the challenges that individuals with behavioural addictions (such as sex addiction and gambling addiction) encounter. Furthermore, impulsivity, sensation-seeking and risk-taking are similar traits in both drug addicts and individuals with behavioural addiction. Therefore, it is safe to say that compulsive behaviours share many similarities with drug addictions. With both substance addiction and behavioural addiction, individuals experience the same impulse control disorder and relapse patterns. Both types of addiction function in the same way as anxiety management; they both result in a "high", and individuals need to escalate their drug or addictive behaviour to get the same euphoric effect due to tolerance building. In both addictions, individuals experience withdrawals.

## Definition Of Addiction

In this regard, the American Society of Addiction Medicine (ASAM, 2011, p. 1) indicated in their *Behavioural Manifestations and Complications of Addiction*, that addiction can present itself in compulsive sexual behaviours (i.e., compulsive pornography use and sex addiction). ASAM defined addiction as:

> *Excessive use and/or engagement in addictive behaviours, at higher frequencies and/or quantities than the person intended, often associated with a persistent desire for and unsuccessful attempts at behavioural control. Excessive time lost in substance use or recovering from the effects of substance use and/or engagement in addictive behaviours, with significant adverse impact on social and occupational functioning (e.g. the development of interpersonal relationship problems or the neglect of responsibilities at home, school, or work). Continued use and/ or engagement in addictive behaviours, despite the presence of persistent or recurrent physical or psychological problems which may have been caused or exacerbated by substance use and/or related addictive behaviours (para. 4).*

CHAPTER 2

# Sex Addiction – An Overview

Compulsive sexual behaviours, hypersexual behaviours, hypersexual disorder and even sexaholic are a few labels given to what is commonly called sex addiction, the preferred term in this book. Authors and health practitioners are yet to agree on standard terminology. Part of the disagreement is about whether sex addiction is actually a disease or a habit. However, there is a consensus regarding the displayed compulsive and unhealthy sexual behaviours in this group of people, regardless of what anyone would like to call the condition. Sex addiction describes the out of control compulsive sexual behaviours and dependency on a mood-altering experience (sex) that the individual continues to engage in – despite severe negative consequences. When these sexual behaviours become a major focus in life, are difficult to manage, and are disruptive or harmful to self or others, they are considered to be symptoms of sex addiction.

Locating sexual partners, while concealing the addictive nature of sexual involvement, may require significant deception. It also reflects a degree of predatory behaviour. Sexual activity might include high levels of fantasy, which may be more important than the activity itself. The sex addict may be "keeping score" about the number of sexual conquests.

There is a common misperception that sex addiction is all about the pursuit of sex and the enjoyment of sexual experiences. Sex addicts are considered to be individuals with high libido, or people who simply like sex too much. They are called nymphomaniacs by some. Another assumption commonly attached to this topic is the sex addict's lack of morality. However, none of these assumptions are correct. Sex addiction has nothing to do with liking sex too much, having an unusually high libido or a misplaced morality. Sex addiction is simply a coping mechanism – a means to avoid real closeness and intimacy – it is a numbing agent, and is based on fear.

Sexual interactions may be limited to a very narrow range of activities. These activities do not foster healthy human relationships. Rather, they replace such relationships or destroy them.

Sex addiction involves a wide range of dysfunctional behaviour: compulsive masturbation, cybersex, participation in chatlines, visitations of strip clubs, brothels or massage parlours, uncontrollable infidelity, and also to a lesser extent, illegal behaviours including exhibitionism and child pornography. These get lumped together under the description "sex addiction" and impact between 3 to 6% of the US population. However, the exact global statistic is difficult to obtain – this is due to the secrecy and shame surrounding the condition. Another current theory is that many sex addicts continue to engage in their compulsive sexual behaviours without realising that they may suffer from addiction. Currently, there are no statistics regarding the exact numbers of sex addicts in Australia.

More and more experts are acknowledging that individuals can become addicted to sex just as they can alcohol, drugs, gambling, and food. Unfortunately, the term "sex addict" or "love addict" sometimes gets a bad rap due to celebrity sex scandals in the media, lack of information, or cheating spouses whose husbands or wives are quick to blame sex addiction for their partner's infidelity. Those who don't have a basic grasp of how the addicted mind operates might turn their nose up at the idea of sex and love addiction. For the sex and love addicts, however, it's much more severe than it might seem on the surface. It can stem from deep-rooted insecurities that range from fear of abandonment to fear of commitment, to fear of intimacy. These insecurities generally result from childhood trauma. The addict's relationship with a mood-altering experience (sex) becomes central to his or her life. Their secret lives become more real than their public lives. What most other people know is purely a false identity. Only the individual addict knows the shame of living a double life – the real world and the secret addict's world. Leading a fantasy double life is a distortion of reality. Online and offline pornography use has been considered a significant cause in the development of compulsive sexual behaviours/sex addiction.

## *Liking sex vs craving sex*

Sex addiction is about experiencing regular release and getting a "fix", similar to a heroin addict, and has nothing to do with true love or intimacy. Research has shown that sex addiction is not about "liking sex more" but about "craving it more". Some sex addicts may find they can't stop thinking about sex and neglect their work to engage in sexual fantasies, preoccupations or activities. Others indulge in sexually risky behaviours, going on "binges" in which they have sex with multiple partners, or pay for prostitutes without any concern given to their current relationship. And still others may feel they have a so-called love addiction and try to fill a void in themselves with sexual activity.

CHAPTER 3

# The Addict's Circle Of Shame

As the addictive behaviours progress, the life of the addict can become more unmanageable. Compulsive sexual behaviours not only have devastating effects on both the life of the addict and others associated with the addict. Marriages are painfully ended. Employment – and even whole careers – are threatened and there can be disastrous financial repercussions. Friendships come to an end. The sex addict struggles to keep the compulsive behaviour in check but is consumed by its destructive nature. An addict's life always revolves around satisfying the addiction (feeding the addiction).

A healthy, non-addicted person who perhaps has made some occasional poor choices in their sex life does not rely on the everyday pursuit of sex. Life doesn't revolve around sex, and sex fills only one aspect of their life. However, the situation is different for a sex addict – sex is the most essential thing each day. For sex addicts, sex is needed to numb the empty emotions they feel inside, and to fill the empty voids in their lives where jobs, people and relationships used to be. They become dependent on sex and are preoccupied with it most days. To get their "fix" (sex) they will not hesitate to lie, manipulate or do whatever it takes. Anyone can make poor life choices at times, but when an individual has lost control and is unable to stop their destructive behaviour, the line has been crossed, boundaries broken, and the occasional poor choice has evolved into a full-blown addiction.

The majority of individuals who engage in compulsive sexual activity are good human beings with a genuine desire to defeat their addiction. Shaming them does not help them – nor make them stop. Non-addicts are able to change their behaviour if they feel guilt or remorse for them. Yet the guilt and shame that prompts the non-addict to change their behaviour will have the opposite effect on a sex addict. He or she feels more ashamed due to their engagement in sexual behaviour, so there will be attempts to relieve the discomfort from imposed shame and distress which leads to even more acting out behaviours. The addict feels shame for their sexual behaviour, which makes them act out even more. It is a circle of shame – the more shame, the more acting-out; the more acting-out, the more shame.

That said, many sex addicts go through recovery successfully and turn their lives around and enter fulfilling and authentic relationships.

# CHAPTER 4

# Pornography

Compulsive use of online and offline pornography is a significant form of sexual addiction.

Online pornography use is on the rise, with its strong potential for sex addiction considering the "triple A" influence of its accessibility, affordability, and anonymity. Negative effects on sexual development and sexual functioning, especially among the younger population, are increasing. This means an inevitable escalation, providing new outlets for established addicts as well as tempting people (due to increased privacy, or opportunity) who would not have previously engaged in these behaviours.

Australian researchers found that in the past year, more than 76% of men and 41% of women had watched pornography. 4% of men and 1% of women reported being addicted. Of these, about half report that pornography has had a bad effect on them, representing a small portion of the sample, but substantial numbers, given that there are well over 20 million people in Australia.

The rise of new technologies has opened up a stream of problematic addictive behaviours, mostly internet pornography addiction. Internet pornography use, or cybersex, is one of those internet-specific behaviours with significant risk for addiction. The use of the internet to engage in various gratifying sexual activities, including viewing pornography, is a popular activity with an infinite number of sexual scenarios. It is a common occurrence that continued use of the internet in this manner causes financial, legal, occupational, and relationship or personal problems, with severe negative ramifications.

## *Internet pornography*

Due to its ability to deliver endless stimulation and activation of the brain's reward system, consumption of internet pornography and related activities can cause supernormal stimulation, where the individual gets caught up in a pathological pursuit. Nikolaas Tinbergen, a Nobel Prize-winning biologist, suggested the idea of "supernormal stimuli", a phenomenon where artificial stimulation can be created which can override a genetic response developed through evolution. To demonstrate this fact, Tinbergen created fake bird's eggs that were larger and more colourful than actual bird's eggs. Remarkably, the mother birds chose to sit on the more vibrant yet artificial eggs and abandon their own naturally laid eggs. Similarly, Tinbergen created artificial butterflies with larger and more colourful wings, and male butterflies repeatedly tried to mate with these artificial butterflies instead of actual female butterflies. In short, according to research, generalised chronic overuse of the internet is highly stimulating. It engages our brains' natural reward system. It potentially activates it at higher levels than the levels of activation our ancestors typically experienced as our brains evolved – making it prone to shift into an addictive mode. In short, online pornography is a "supranormal stimulus" similar in effect to an actual substance (i.e. heroin) through continued consumption, and can spark an addictive disorder.

## *Hooked on pornography*

Current research reveals that pornography acts like a drug in the brain of some people and causes the same areas of the brain to be activated – similar to the effects of drugs, nicotine and alcohol. The brains of sex addicts have been found to have more reactivities in comparison to healthy individuals. Therefore, watching pornography, particularly when it becomes habitual or compulsive, can activate the same brain network/neuropathways. This is similar to how the consumption of alcohol and other drugs impact the brain's reactivity.

## *Exposure to pornography and sexual development in younger ages*

An Australian study found that almost 44% of children aged 9–16 had viewed pornographic images in the previous month. This study further found that 16% of these kids had viewed images of others engaging in sexual acts and 17% had seen somebody else's genitals. Exposure to adult pornography can cause distress and upset to younger children (commonly between the ages of 9–12). Other research found that parents often underestimate the exposure to pornography for the older children while overestimating the exposure to younger children. Older teens tend to view pornography as amusing, arousing or exciting. There are also some gender differences, with males more likely to deliberately and more frequently seek out pornography. Females have been found to have more negative, views, attitudes and reactions to pornography in comparison to males. These negative reactions include shock, distress and low relationship satisfaction.

Youthful pornography use has been linked with stronger beliefs in gender stereotypes, particularly for males. Adolescents who consume violent pornography are six times more likely to be sexually aggressive compared to those who viewed non-violent pornography or no pornography. We know that a considerable proportion of the young male population access the internet for the consumption of pornography; in fact, it is a key source in their sexual awareness. Some have expressed concern about this, addressing the time gap between when porn material is consumed for the first time, and an actual first sexual experience. Specifically, areas of concern include how the former (exposure to porn at an early age) can have an impact on sexual development. Effects may be abnormally low sexual desire when consuming online pornography, and erectile dysfunction, which has spiked dramatically among young men in the past few years when compared to a couple of decades ago.

## *The effects of exposure*

Use of pornography in adolescence is commonly linked with stronger liberal sexual attitudes (e.g. casual sex, one-night stands and sex before marriage). According to research, exposure to pornography is associated with the likelihood of earlier first-time sexual experiences, especially for those who use pornography more frequently. Pornography can impact a young individual's expectations about sex and intimacy; for example, young men's expectations of their partner's behaviour in bed and vice versa. Some studies find that young people may even attempt performing sexual acts viewed in dominant heterosexual pornographic images. The consumption of pornography by teenagers has been associated with unsafe sexual health practices e.g. not using condoms, unplanned pregnancies, sexually transmitted diseases, and unsafe anal and vaginal sexual acts. Viewing pornography can lead to unrealistic gaps between learned expectations and reality, "sexual uncertainty" about sexual attitudes, beliefs and values; decreased sexual satisfaction and increased anxiety and fear.

Additionally, pornographic content may emphasise stereotyped standards: an active male sexuality with females as passive receptacles. It is known that both male and female consumers of pornography have higher levels of objectification and self-objectification. Male pornography users are more likely to view and treat women as sex objects, and some hold sexist attitudes, such as the false accusation of women "leading men on". Other very concerning negative influences of the consumption of pornography include the support for and strengthening of sexually violent attitudes – particularly against women. The association between pornography consumption and acts of sexual harassments have long been observed.

Other negative issues associated with pornography are substantial, including misuse of sex industry workers and human trafficking, child pornography, pornography addiction, problematic influences on our views of sexuality and social relationships, and interference with bonding and attachment in romantic relationships – as well as contributing to the general objectification of, primarily, women, but also men.

**Cybersex** is engaging in sexually addictive thoughts, fantasies or behaviour over the internet rather than in person, and is another form of sex addiction. Although this is difficult to accurately determine given the anonymity, affordability and accessibility factors that make pornography use today so inescapable, we know at least that the behaviour of the consumer of pornography has changed in the last decade. Recent studies agree this behaviour is an addiction with important clinical manifestations, such as sexual dysfunction and relationship dissatisfaction. Therefore, claiming that internet pornography is not addictive and not a major problem is simply a mistake. It is of major significance because of how it erodes the physical and emotional intimacy in real relationships. Because:

- **Pornography creates unrealistic expectations and attitudes about the role of an intimate partner and sexual behaviours.** Studies have found that frequent pornography use in committed relationships can create false impressions of what an average body should look like, and can undermine the commitment within the relationship. Pornographic images commonly revolve around self-gratification, control, domination, or performers who are very eager to satisfy, or overly submissive. In contrast, a healthy sexual relationship is about a mutually satisfying expression of partners' love for each other.

- **Healthy relationships are based on mutual trust.** To be intimate with someone requires vulnerability, and trust is the guarantee that the private partner will respect and honour that vulnerability. When a partner engages in secret encounters with others, and is unfaithful to the exclusive, sacred nature of a relationship, it shatters the trust, and feelings of betrayal and violation commonly follow. Destruction of trust requires a long time and much intentional hard work to rebuild.

- **Emotional intimacy is needed to create an authentic and long-lasting relationship.** However, if a person takes all their relationship cues from internet pornography sites, or even from the other relentless messages streaming through the media, they may solely focus on sexual intimacy and wrongly believe that sex is the necessary primary binding agent in relationships. When emotional intimacy is present in a relationship, partners will feel valued, cherished, appreciated, listened to, cared for and loved. Consequently, sexual intimacy and satisfaction within such a relationship are significantly greater. Pornography consumption is associated with lower emotional commitment amongst both men and women, with a higher effect on men.

- **Pornography viewing early in the relationship is a predictor for a greater chance of romantic breakup later on.** Research has found men who consume pornography experience more relationship dissatisfaction, sexual infidelity and loss of attachment to their romantic partner. Other causes for the breakup of romantic relationships could be that partners of pornography consumers often feel inadequate, resentful, betrayed and abandoned and unable to compete with the pornographic images which can lead to low self-esteem and relationship dissatisfaction. What researchers have discovered is that using pornography can affect the viewer by giving them the (false) impression that there are many potential sexual partners available, which in turn may lower their dedication to their intimate partner.

- **Using pornography can lead to the desire to swap out the real partner who is actually in the bed with a fantasy person who has been viewed on the screen.** Pornography consumption can increase the desire for fantasy alternatives, which can cause real-world infidelity and cheating. As just mentioned, this is because viewing physically attractive and sexually available partners on screen can distort and alter the viewer's perceptions of alternative and available possible partners. Individuals who consume pornography may also find multiple sexual partners more desirable which again can cause profound harm to a committed partner/relationship. Many heavy porn users have difficulties feeling aroused in bed with a real partner without fantasising about pornographic images, and report performance anxiety/inability when attempting to avoid such images or fantasies.

- **Secrecy and dishonesty about pornography use can cause general mistrust and insecurity in the relationship.** According to research, female partners of male pornography users tend to value and trust their partners and relationships less. On the other hand, people who do not use pornography tend to have higher levels of effective communications and sexual satisfaction within a committed dyad. At the same time, their rate of infidelity has been found to be at least half of those who have watched sexual material alone and with their partners. Consumers of pornography have shown to be more likely to engage in flirting behaviour outside their committed relationships, and more likely to cheat and hook-up with others.

- **Pornography addiction and erectile dysfunction.** Recent studies found that for some their inability to perform sexually will only affect them when they are intimate with their real partner, while they can perform using pornographic materials or with random partners. This problem is becoming widespread among many young individuals addicted to pornography and compulsive masturbation. These individuals are trapped and unable to perform with real partners when the opportunity presents itself.

- **Erectile dysfunction may have many contributing factors, one of these being compulsive pornography use.** Studies in support of the link between pornography and erectile dysfunction argue that heavy porn consumption can desensitise sexual response. A recent study found that more young men are currently facing this condition. Other studies found that pornography use may lower men's body image satisfaction and self-esteem while increasing anxiety during sexual performance. Compulsive use of pornography can alter the brain's reactivity to arousal, and lower sexual satisfaction and excitement with a real partner. Some may even experience lower libido and need increased sexual stimulation (escalation) to feel and remain sexually aroused.

As discussed, engaging in compulsive online and offline pornography viewing is a supernormal stimulus of the brain circuitry. This could be caused due to the availability and affordability of pornography, and the anonymity of its consumption, which allows the individual continuously and instantly to self-select novel and more sexually arousing images. This, in turn, has the power to increase a person's "tolerance" and need for "more" – the same process as with drug addiction. With time, regular and real-world sexual images will less likely appeal to habitual/compulsive porn viewers, and they must increase their reliance on pornography for desired effect and release.

This explains why regular porn users are affected by sexual dysfunction and display a preference for pornography over partnered sex.

Many sex addicts are unable to perform with real partners yet achieve arousal through online or offline activities.

Researchers discovered that a person's high exposure to pornographic materials resulted in lower responsivity and an increased need for more extreme, specialized or "kinky" material to become aroused. Since then, evidence has mounted that internet pornography may be a factor in the rapid surge in rates of sexual dysfunction and sex addictions.

A 2015 study of men (average age 41.5) seeking treatment for hypersexuality, who masturbated (typically with widespread pornography use) seven or more hours per week, found that 71% had sexual dysfunctions, with 33% reporting difficulty orgasming.

In 2014, Bronner and Ben-Zion observed the results of when a compulsive internet pornography user sought treatment for decreased sexual desire during partnered sex. He had escalated his behaviour to extreme hardcore pornography – with loss of appeal to regular pornography. Only after eight months of discontinuing all exposure to pornography and compulsive sexual acting out, did the patient report experiencing successful orgasm and ejaculation and succeed in enjoying relational sex.

Similarly, in another study, 11 of 19 participants who were compulsive internet pornography users (average age 25), had their brains scanned for evidence of addiction. These people reported that due to excessive internet pornography consumption they had experienced reduced libido or increased erectile dysfunction, particularly when in physical relationships with women. However, these people did not report these experiences in connection with sexually explicit material.

## *Escalation*

Norman Doidge in his highly regarded book on neuroplasticity, *The Brain That Changes Itself*, reviewed the current research on addiction and the brain's reward system. He observed that the continued release of *dopamine* (which impacts how we feel pleasure and gives us the human ability to think and plan) into the brain's reward system occurs when an individual compulsively and chronically watches internet pornography, or engages in compulsive sexual acts. This actually encourages *neuroplasticity changes* (the ability of neural networks in the brain to change) which, in turn, reinforce the experience.

Doidge further described how these neuroplastic alterations shape brain maps for sexual excitement and arousal. Because of his observations he was able to introduce an additional element of tolerance; previously recognised brain maps for "natural" sexuality cannot relate to the newly developed and continuously reinforced maps generated by continued compulsive watching of internet pornography. He indicated that the addicted individual progresses and escalates in their behaviours towards more explicit and graphic internet pornography to maintain required higher levels of arousal and excitement.

Currently, there are available screening tools for online pornography assessment, and the most-often used screening tool is the Internet Sex-Screening Test (ISST). It assesses five distinct dimensions (online sexual compulsivity, online sexual behaviour-social, online sexual behaviour-isolated, online sexual spending and interest in online sexual behaviour) through 25 dichotomic (yes/no) questions regarding online and offline pornography use.

To take the test visit:

Dr. Fai Seyed Aghamiri

http://www.recoveryzone.com/tests/sex-addiction/ISST/index.php

or

https://psychology-tools.com/test/internet-addiction-assessment

# CHAPTER 5

# Addiction To Masturbation

Pornography-related masturbation is a behaviour that is on the rise. Although not everyone who masturbates is an addict, when this behaviour becomes compulsive, obsessive and excessive, then the individual has a sexual addiction. You know you have formed an unhealthy dependency on masturbation when:

- Masturbation takes up a great deal of your time and attention.
- Your personal, professional or academic performance is suffering because of it.

- You must rearrange, cancel or leave occupational or social appointments because of it.
- You feel irritable and anxious when cravings come.
- Masturbation becomes a comfort when you have negative emotions or feel stressed, anxious, or as a means to help you to fall asleep.
- You feel the need to continue engaging in the behaviour while keeping it a secret, and feel ashamed of your behaviour being exposed to loved ones.
- You are unable to discontinue for a long period of time.
- You feel ashamed or regretful after masturbating.
- You are preoccupied with thoughts of masturbation.
- You feel the urge even when you do not feel sexually aroused.
- You may masturbate in public or workplaces because you cannot resist the urges or wait to get home.

CHAPTER 6

# Similarities With Other Addictions

Sexual behaviour activates the same "reward system" circuitry in the brain as addictive drugs, such as cocaine and methamphetamines, which can result in self-reinforcing activity, or recurrent behaviours. As mentioned, current studies found that although sex addiction does not depend on external chemicals it is similar to other addictions, and similar to drugs and alcohol. It is known that a sex addict may experience a high (like a drug high) from their own brain chemistry. For a sex addict the brain activity could be triggered by watching pornography. Engaging in sexual fantasies, acts or pornography consumption causes brain chemical changes and stimulates dopamine release. Dopamine is responsible for people getting high on drugs such as cocaine and on heroin. In sex addicts, the drug that causes the high is sex, which acts similarly to drugs and activates the brain's reward system. Sex addiction can be considered the brain's chemical dependency. The individuals do not *like* sex more – their brain just *craves* it more.

Sex addicts crave sex more and depend on it for euphoric pleasure. For sex addicts, sex has little to do with intimacy or love. Instead, it is all about escapism and avoidance from painful or distressing emotions. They use sex as a way to self-medicate and numb unpleasant emotions. Identical to the alcoholic, compulsive gambler, or drug addict, sex addicts are focused and at times obsessed with the desire to get their next fix – no matter how high the risks and potential negative implications. Sex addicts are stuck in the same vicious cycle of indulgence in compulsive sexual behaviours, feeling guilt, shame and remorse, while promising themselves to change. Only to find themselves giving in to the cravings all over again. This is identical to other type of addictions.

These observed similarities between the cycle of sex addiction and other addictions are reasons why more experts are agreeing that some people are genuinely addicted to sex. Drug addicts and sex addicts share a pleasurable feeling and high due to the chemical changes in the brain. In an attempt to enhance the high, or to cope or escape the shame after acting out, some sex addicts may also turn to other addictions such as drugs, gambling, gaming or compulsive spending. Cross addiction is common in sex addicts. However, the vicious cycle of addiction can be broken.

Unlike the effect of drugs, most healthy people do not become addicted to the brain chemicals released when sexually intimate with another person. However, individuals who have experienced childhood trauma, abuse, neglect or abandonment, attachment

## Similarities With Other Addictions

wounds or lived in a dysfunctional family system have the potential to develop unhealthy attachments to compulsive sexual behaviours. These individuals appear to react with anxiety or disproportionate agitation when they do not receive what they perceive as love or connection, which is sex. Sexual release becomes a way of anxiety management for them. Although sex and love addiction are not universally recognised as diseases, the fact remains that many individuals severely struggle with out-of-control sexual behaviours, and their lives are unmanageable. Furthermore, families and society are negatively impacted too.

CHAPTER 7

# The Brain And Sex Addiction

Sex addiction changes and impairs optimal brain functioning. Brain science tells us that instead of wanting that which will enhance survival, the addicted are motivated to want – even when it is clearly harmful – a neuroplastic process [i.e. brain change] *that recalibrates the hedonistic set point. And: "We can now see addiction, whether to smoking, cocaine, or sex, through the lens of the neural receptor and subsequent neuroplastic change, and not solely from a behavioural perspective"* (Hatch 2019, para. 2)

*In other words, there is reason to believe that addicted individuals have a learned but illogical motivation toward an experience (sex) or substance, and that that exaggerated desire or craving becomes their brain's new normal.* (ibid, para. 5).

These changes in the brain due to compulsive sexual activities or pornography use impact the executive functioning of the brain. The specifics of this poorer executive functioning include impulsivity, cognitive rigidity that affects learning processes or the ability to shift attention, poor judgement and decision making, interference of working memory capacity, deficits in emotion regulation, and excessive preoccupation with sex. Finally, it is clear that the networks involved in human sexual behaviour are remarkably similar to the networks involved in processing other rewards.

Studies have found that both masturbation and online and offline compulsive sexual activities could blend themselves, stating that men use it as an almost limitless extension of an out of control masturbatory behaviour. Others have shown that sex addiction is a steady transition from voluntary actions to habitual actions to compulsive actions due to the shift in the brain reward system. Gambling, shopping, gaming, food and sex activate and extend amygdala in the same manner as do drugs of abuse. Extensive data suggest that eating, shopping, gambling, playing video games, and spending time on the internet are behaviours that can develop into compulsive/addictive behaviours that are continued, despite devastating consequences. Men appear to outnumber women with compulsive sexual behaviours.

Sex addicts, when in the state of craving that experience (sex), are stuck in a part of their brain that is cut off from the reasoning power to restrain their impulse. The link between drug addiction and sexual addiction makes it clear that sexual addiction is not really about morality or even sex, but is driven by the same compulsion to stimulate the brain's reward system by engaging in reckless, destructive behaviour. As discussed, sexual activity (like the effects of alcohol, drugs, and gambling), increases levels of dopamine in the brain.

The brain considers sex as an activity intrinsic to the survival of the species, and the activity is rewarded by the release of dopamine which promotes a pleasurable euphoria. However, this mechanism of the brain's reward system makes individuals vulnerable to addiction. As mentioned before, people do not actually become addicted to sex, but similar to all addictions, the true dependence is on the release of brain chemicals that occur during compulsive behaviour (sex).

There are brain changes in addicts that make it harder for them to resist cravings and avoid relapse. However, the good news is that those brain changes can be reversed.

## *Binge and purge*

One of the fundamental hallmarks of sex addiction is continued engagement in sexual activities – despite the negative consequences created by these activities. This is the same phenomenon seen in substance abuse and impulse control disorders. Psychologically, sexual behaviours serve to escape emotional or physical pain or are a way of dealing with life stressors. The irony is that sexual behaviours become the primary way of coping and handling problems that, in turn, creates a cycle of more problems and increasing desperation, shame, and preoccupation. Most addicts (72%) binge and then feel despair – much like a person with bulimia will binge and purge. For example, a number of clergymen preach against promiscuity or some sexual behaviour only to be discovered engaging in or arrested for that behaviour. In their public pronouncements, they were purging, while privately they were clearly binging. Sex addicts can go through periods of total abstinence and then enter a binge phase in their compulsive sexual activities.

# CHAPTER 8

# Cycles Of Sex Addiction, according to Dr Patrick Carnes, are as follows:

***First Stage – Preoccupation***

When sex addicts have feelings that go unresolved, they seek to control. They try to handle the sentiments by making them go away. Sex addicts turn to fantasies and preoccupations, and this "trance-like" state is the beginning of the addictive cycle. Fantasies are a way for the sex addict to numb themself, a form of self-medication that provides a temporary release from the suffering/pain that may define much of their life.

The person becomes a hostage to his or her own thoughts as they try to escape from pain, negative self-evaluation and fear of others' judgements. Sex addiction, as mentioned earlier, is about escaping uncomfortable emotions and numbing them. Most sex addicts find early on that they are able to manage the intensity of this numbness by participating in specific rituals and sexual behaviours. These behaviours start with sexual fantasies and preoccupations, which become more intense, until they evolve into harmful behaviours. These unhealthy and harmful behaviours gradually become more intense. They become less effective over time, compelling the individuals to invest more time and energy into them to achieve the desired relief. It is not about merely noticing sexually attractive people, rather there is a quality of desperation that affects the sex addict's occupation, relaxation, and even impacts their sleep. For a sex addict in this desperate stage, people turn into objects to be scrutinised. Observing people in busy city malls or other public places give the sex addict's brain an infinite shopping list of possibilities.

A sex addict learns through compulsive and repeated sexual fantasies and acts to use and abuse one of the most sacred and exciting moments in human existence: sex. As the sexual arousal is intensified, the addict enters into an obsessive trance-like state and his or her mood changes. The brain's chemicals are rushing through the body and increasing bodily functioning while the heart starts pounding as the addict focuses more on the sexual object. There are increased risks, danger and even violence as the fundamental escalators. The trance-like state and preoccupations numb the shame and personal pain. Even thinking or anticipating acting out is enough to bring relief and works as stress management. This could explain why sex addicts do not need to act out every time.

The preoccupation stage is frequently referred to as the craving stage, when there is a lack of dopamine due to malfunctioning of dopamine-producing nerve cells.

This leaves the individual vulnerable to repeat the compulsive behaviours. Two primary mechanisms that are impaired have been identified: cue-induced reinstatement and stress-induced reinstatement. These impairments are the source behind "chronic relapsing".

Patrick Carnes talks about the "hijacked brain". It is like running late for an appointment. All the person can focus on is getting where they need to go; there's no other reality. When the sex addict is in this state, others become objects to be judged, sexualised, pursued, hunted, sought, and checked upon. Misperceptions occur mistaking intensity for intimacy, obsession for caring, and control for security.

Gradually, addicts become more dependent on these fantasies and preoccupations to receive relief from negative self-evaluation, fear of others' judgement and to achieve emotional numbness. In this stage the sex addict turns into a hostage to their own compulsive thoughts, and their brain seems to be hijacked. At this stage, ability to invest time and effort into seeking alternative ways to peace become impossible. This leads to the second stage, ritualization.

## *Second Stage – Ritualization*

This consists of special routines that are created to intensify the preoccupation, which adds arousal, excitement and a sense of control. The rituals include but are not limited to cruising, choice of clothing and/or music, browsing the internet, participating on chatlines, cleaning the house in order to create the right "vibe" to act out in, etc. The rituals can be a further distraction from feelings of being unloved and worthless. The objects of these rituals are the first step down a familiar path towards the behaviours sex addicts are compelled to complete, though in their hearts they do not want to.

Ritualization involves following routines that strengthen and intensify the preoccupations. This stage further enhances and supports the trance state. The addict enters a state that is difficult to break willingly where they do not have to stop, think or interrupt their behaviour. The first two phases of the sexual addiction cycle (preoccupation and ritualization) may not be easily detectable but both stimulate a dopamine rush and enhance the euphoric and excitement state.

This ritualization (repeated routines) causes the addict to forget about the severe consequences of their actions. Some of the ritualization behaviours include browsing the internet, watching porn, cruising the streets where the strip clubs or sex workers are, engaging in chatlines or phone sex. Most addicts exist in a double life while they struggle more and more to control the compulsive behaviours.

Acting out or compulsive sexual behaviours is the third stage and here the addict faces the problematic actions.

## *Third Stage – Acting Out*

The actual acting out phase is the shortest in the cycle. The behaviours include, but are not limited to, affairs, compulsive masturbation, pornography addiction, cybersex, secrecy, exhibitionism, voyeurism (the practice of gaining sexual pleasure from watching others when they are naked or engaged in sexual activity), indecent calls or touch, strip clubs, erotic massages, visiting sex workers and anonymous sex. It is true that addicts before recovery are powerless over their behaviours.

When individuals have reached a point where they have lost control over their sexual expression, they are called addicts. The fact that these individuals have failed to control their compulsive behaviours is a sign of their true addiction. Sex addicts often designate a specific day, such as a child's birthday, a change of occupation, a holiday or an anniversary as "the last day", when they will stop acting out. There are numerous occasions when an addict promises him or herself to stop engaging in compulsive acts. They even set a goal, a day, or a year. However, it does not take long before these promises and goals fail and addicts find themselves powerless and experiencing yet again a loss of self-control, bad morality and increased shame. However, with help, education and non-judgmental support these individuals can break free from their addiction.

## *Fourth Stage – Shame and Despair*

The brief moment of relief when engaging in a sexual act quickly fades, and all the addict is left with is a pit of despair and self-loathing. Despair is utter hopelessness, sadness, desperation and fear over one's powerlessness. They often ask themselves "Why do I keep doing this?" A warped belief system responds "because you are weak", "because you are low value", "because you are worthless". Their thoughts sink them deeper and deeper into a pit of suffering, reinforcing these flawed beliefs, and they seek a way out, beginning the cycle all over again. The cycle becomes a vicious one when the sense of failing oneself and others, and not keeping promises, begins to erode and further damage the person's integrity and self-esteem. This is when hopelessness and helplessness move in, which can be avoided by going back to the preoccupation state, thus repeating the cycle. The reprieve from this despair, which in the worst case can lead to suicidal thoughts, is enough to keep addicts acting compulsively.

Most sex addicts quickly learn to wall much of their behaviour off and ignore it.

This is an attempt for the addicts to keep themselves separated from the reality of being in a state of unmanageability. The primary relationship for a sex addict is sexual, and their reason for being revolves around sexual experiences. Sexual experiences for a sex addict are the sources of euphoria, excitement, nurturing and motivation.

Sex addicts learn to use sex as pain relief, for anxiety management, the reward for success and for emotional regulation. Commonly sex addicts do not know how to feel their emotions, rather trying to escape them through sexual activity. There are ongoing internal tensions in the addict's world. There is a normal person and an addict within the same body; a Jekyll/Hyde struggle exists. Relatives of sex addicts are often left in disbelief when exposed to the truth of the sex addict's double life. After all, sex addiction cannot be sensed on the breath like alcohol, or observed in the obvious signs of drug abuse. Sex addicts can hide their behaviour for years without getting caught. The addictive system is so forceful that addicts cannot simply stop. Generally, a sex addict must hit rock bottom, experience a major crisis or be discovered to create the situation when he or she is prepared to stop the denial and get help.

Understanding the sex addiction cycle and behaviours, recognising the triggers and learning to self-regulate are the first steps towards breaking the cycle and effective recovery. True recovery can lead to relief from guilt and shame and the ability to form healthy relationships.

# CHAPTER 9

# Signs Of Sex Addiction

Some indications that the individual may be struggling with compulsive sexual behaviours/sex addiction include:
- Recurrent and intense sexual fantasies, urges and behaviours that take up a lot of the person's time, and where they feel out of control and powerless.
- Feeling driven to act out certain sexual behaviours, feeling a release of the tension afterwards, but also feeling guilt, shame or remorse.
- Escalation – needing to make the behaviour more intense, more frequent, or riskier.
- Attempting unsuccessfully to reduce or control sexual fantasies, urges or behaviours.

- Use of compulsive sexual behaviours as an escape from other problems, such as loneliness, depression, anxiety or stress.
- Engaging in sexual acts that have severe negative implications, including loss of meaningful relationships, occupational, financial or legal problems and contracting or transferring a sexually transmitted infection.
- Losses – losing, limiting, or sacrificing valued parts of life such as hobbies, family, relationships, and work.
- Difficulties in establishing and maintaining healthy and stable relationships.
- Staying up late.
- Looking at pornography.
- Frequently isolating from spouses or partners, and not informing them of their whereabouts, and seeming disconnected.
- Reduced academic or occupational performance, and seeming preoccupied.
- Controlling behaviour during sex or demanding sex and offering no appropriate communication during sex.
- Becoming angry or defensive if someone shows concern about a problem with pornography.
- Lacking intimacy before, during and after sex, in a relationship.
- Attempting to switch to other forms of pornography or sexual behaviours.
- Feeling depressed.
- Increased secrecy with passwords or text messages.
- Increased dishonesty and gaslighting.
- Hiding pornography at work or at home.
- Lacking close friends of the same sex.
- Frequently flirting or using sexual humour or language.
- Always having a good reason for looking at pornography.
- Withdrawal – stopping sex addict behaviour causes considerable distress, anxiety, restlessness, irritability, or physical discomfort.

## *Causes and Risk Factors*

**Availability and ease of access to online and offline pornography and sexually gratifying materials.** Thanks to the internet, access to porn is a click away.

**Privacy** – viewing porn in private is easier than ever. Sex addiction activities thrive in secrecy. In a study of 932 sex addicts in 2013, 90% of men and 77% of women indicated that pornography played a significant role in their addiction.

**Trauma and abuse during childhood** – according to some research, a high percentage of individuals (over 80%) with an addiction to sex have a history of being abused during childhood. Sex addicted individuals often have a history of sexual abuse, physical abuse, and emotional abuse and suffer from post-traumatic stress disorder (PTSD). Addictions become a way to manage their stress disorder and may include repeating the trauma compulsively.

- 97% experienced emotional abuse
- 81% experienced sexual abuse
- 72% experienced physical abuse

One study found that survivors of chronic childhood trauma (four or more significant trauma experiences before age 18) are:

- 8 times as likely to smoke cigarettes
- 9 times as likely to become obese
- 4 times as likely to experience ongoing anxiety
- 6 times as likely to be depressed
- 6 times as likely to qualify as promiscuous
- Twice as likely to become alcoholic
- One time more likely to become an intravenous drug user.

**Nurture/family attachment:** Among sex addicts a family history of drug abuse and the presence of addiction are common occurrences. Another common element is dysfunctional family systems, particularly where parents were emotionally unavailable, rigid, abusive or uncaring in their parenting style. Those struggling with sexual compulsivity typically have a long history of unmet needs and emotional suffering.

Depending on the caregivers, most sex addicts have been raised in homes with rigid, non-existent or chaotic **personal boundaries**. Nurturing and connection are normal requirements during childhood. For most sex addicts these needs were not met, were ignored or deemed "unworthy" by narcissistic or dysfunctional caregivers. At times the child had to "parent" the caregiver or meet the parents' needs and ignore their own. When a child's needs are not met or they are ignored, the child thinks his or her needs are "wrong". This is how many abused children feel and end up blaming themselves for being wrong and the reason for not getting love or attention. Gradually, as the child's needs are trampled on or ignored, a mask of "normalcy" may be created as a way to cope with the dysfunctional system. Behind this mask is a child who has learned to please, lie, manipulate, isolate and act out to get what she or he badly needs. These coping strategies become maladaptive behaviours and function as inferior signals of the addict's true needs. Gradually, the true self shrinks while the false self behind the mask grows larger and stronger.

At some point in the sex addict's life, sexual behaviours became a way to feel better. These sexual behaviours become addicts' coping mechanisms because the experience of having needs met in a consistent, intimate way from the adults around them was missing. Abused and/or neglected children are incredibly at risk for addiction (and other adult life psychological issues) regardless of genetic influences. And the more times a child is traumatized, the greater the likelihood of adverse reactions, such as addiction, later in life.

**Early exposure to sexual activities:** another relatively common environmental risk factor is early exposure to an addictive substance or behaviour. Numerous studies tell us that the lower the age of first use, the higher the likelihood of addiction. This is true with all forms of addiction, including sexual addiction. Whether sex was vilified or glorified, a large percentage of sex addicts were exposed to it at an unusually early age.

**Biochemical imbalances:** sexual stimulation and response are functions of both the brain and the genitals. Sexual release is a way to temporarily self-medicate the imbalance; repeated sexual acts leads to more imbalance and the need for more stimulation. Compulsive behaviours are known to be linked with imbalances of certain brain chemical called neurotransmitters. Some of these neurotransmitters include dopamine, serotonin, and norepinephrine that assist with mood regulation and play a role in the experience of euphoria and pleasure. The intense euphoria experienced by the sex addict during acting out can partially be caused by high levels of these chemicals. These chemicals have the potential of becoming addictive.

Understanding brain chemicals and how they impact the brain can sometimes make certain medications useful in treating sex addiction. These medications include antidepressants (e.g., SSRIs, Selective Serotonin Reuptake Inhibitors), that have been found to be beneficial for treating sex addicts because they target serotonin. Other useful medications in this context are mood stabilisers such as lithium. However, not every sex addict needs medication and thorough assessment during the recovery process is essential. Although use of some medications in treating sex addiction has proved successful, other studies have shown that certain medications, such as dopamine agonists (sometimes used to treat Parkinson's disease) may actually lead to compulsive sexual behaviour.

**Medical conditions** or other types of addictions: dementia, multiple sclerosis and Huntington's disease are some of the medical conditions that damage certain regions of the brain. This damage could contribute to compulsive sexual behaviours. Other co-occurring psychiatric disorders, such as depression, bipolar disorder, a personality disorder (e.g. narcissistic personality disorder or borderline personality disorder), a substance abuse problem or another type of addiction (including a gambling addiction) may increase the risk of development of compulsive sexual behaviours.

**Hormones:** both men and women have sex hormones known as androgens. Increased release of **dopamine** and **androgen** due to high stimulation can lead to addiction. Dopamine dysfunction leads to more tolerance and an increased need for stimulation. Androgens affect libido and, if overstimulated, can play a role in a person's addiction to sex.

Medications that affect hormones are sometimes used in the treatment of sex addicts. These include anti-androgens and LHRH (luteinizing hormone-releasing hormone) agonists. Anti-androgens help decrease sexual urges. LHRH agonists lower testosterone production and may help with the sexual obsessions that often accompany this addiction. Both medications are often used to treat male paedophiles and other types of male sex offenders.

**Genetics:** it is believed that through genetic predisposition, many genes contribute towards the development of sexual addiction. Genetics may explain why some individuals are more vulnerable to sex addiction compared to others.

For example, the research found pathological gamblers to be three times more likely to have a parent who is a pathological gambler, and twelve times more likely to have a grandparent. Genetic research revealed that children of alcoholics to be 50%–60% more likely to become alcoholics. The same is true with certain heritable personality traits, like impulsivity, risk-taking, and novelty-seeking.

Genetic factors have been found to also indirectly contribute to addiction. For examples, with many psychiatric disorders such as depression, anxiety, attention deficits, bipolar disorder, social phobia etc., genetics are an important factor. Notably, individuals living with these health challenges end up self-medicating with alcohol, drugs, sex and/or addictive behaviour.

In other words, what is considered genetically inherited is not an exceptional reaction to a potentially addictive drug or behaviour, but the tendency for an underlying neurobiological weakness or susceptibility that could, gradually, lead to addiction.

**Changes in neural pathways due to repeated sexual activities:** due to repeated compulsive behaviours the brain's neural pathway (which is brain's complex wiring system) can be altered.

Compulsive sexual behaviour over time can cause changes in the brain's neural circuits, especially in the reinforcement centres of the brain. As discussed, like other addictions, more intensive sexual content and stimulation are typically required over time to gain satisfaction or relief. These alterations promote the pleasure and euphoria experienced during sexual activity. Consequently, this makes it more difficult to overcome the addiction because of the unpleasant reactions (withdrawals) when individuals attempt to discontinue the behaviours.

## *Screening tools*

*Sex addiction can be assessed by using the Sexual Addiction Screening Test (SAST) proposed by Patrick Carnes, which was later revised to version SAST-R. The Sexual Addiction Screening Test (SAST) is designed to assist in the assessment of sexually compulsive behaviour which may indicate the presence of sex addiction and provides a profile of responses which help to discriminate between addictive and non-addictive behaviour. However, these tools all rely on the respondent's honesty and integrity – perhaps even more so than regular psychiatric screening tests, since sexual practices are the most humbling to reveal due to their private nature.*

# CHAPTER 10

# The Addict's Belief System

To understand how the addiction begins and how progressively insanity appears, it is good to know that it begins with the delusional thought processes engrained in the addict's belief system. Dr Patrick Carnes suggests that addicts commonly start with core beliefs about themselves that influence how they experience and perceive reality. The belief system for every individual is the total assumptions, judgements, and myths that he or she holds to be true. This includes compelling family messages about an individual's value or worth, relationships, needs, and sexuality. Internally, it is a range of what "options" – answers, ideas, potentials, ways of acting are available to each person. This forms the foundation and model of how a person views the world. This model assists the individuals to:

- Make plans and decisions
- Make sense and interpretations of other's actions
- Make certain meaning out of life experiences
- Solve problems
- Build relationships
- Cultivate and progress in their careers
- Determine priorities
- Make choices affecting their lives.

The core elements of a sex addict's belief system are faulty and inaccurate which paves the way for the development of addiction. Sex addiction is strongly anchored in the addict's core beliefs. Addicts commonly suffer from low self-worth, increased shame, and consider themselves to be unworthy failures. Sex addicts believe that no one would care for them or meet their needs particularly if they were exposed. They strongly believe that sex is their fundamental need and the only thing that makes their isolation bearable. Their relationship is formed with sex and not with people. People are not trustworthy. Their lack of trust in others makes the sexual acts appealing because it helps them escape the pain, however momentarily.

## *Impaired Thinking and Rationalisation*

Individuals' fundamental beliefs about themselves and the world are formed in childhood, and they shape and guide them throughout life. When they are warped, so are individuals, and so are their lives and realities. Because of the addict's faulty belief system, the views of reality become twisted and distorted. Through denial to self and others about problems, the addict learns to distort reality. Disregarding the problem, shifting the blame to others, and minimising the destructive behaviours are part of the addict's defensive behaviours. Sex addicts contribute the consequences (such as unplanned pregnancy, loss of relationships or job or legal problems) of their behaviours to factors other than addiction. **They either minimise, deflect, shift blame or deny problems.**

Dr Patrick Carnes in his book *Out of the Shadows: Understanding Sexual Addiction* described some of this impaired thinking and rationalisations:

- *Venereal disease: "A lot of people get it now."*
- *Pregnancy: "She tricked me into it."*
- *Arrests: "Cops had it in for me. They had no real proof."*
- *Jobs: "The boss needs to be liberated."*
- *Relationships: "Her family always had problems. She simply couldn't handle it."*

*When addicts believe in these defensive rationalisations, the result is denial that a specific incident or behaviour is a part of a total behavioural pattern. Arguments, excuses, justifications, and circular reasoning abound in the addict's impaired mental processes:*

- *If I don't have it every few days, the pressure builds up.*
- *Masturbation is normal, everyone does it.*
- *I am oversexed and have to meet my needs.*
- *What she doesn't know won't hurt her.*
- *My husband is not sensitive to my needs.*
- *She really enjoyed it, asked for it, deserved it, got paid.*
- *Only certain men turn me on, and my husband isn't one of them.*
- *Every guy will get what "nookie" he can.*

- *If only my wife would be more responsive.*
- *Men are like animals – males are more sexual than females.*
- *Cybersex is just electrons; it's not real.*
- *With the stress I am under, I deserve it.*
- *It doesn't hurt anybody because . . .*
- *The internet helps to broaden my sexual horizons.*
- *I couldn't help it, given how she acted.*
- *No one really cares.*
- *It's my way of relaxing.*
- *Internet chat rooms don't hurt anybody – it's just a game.*
- *Women always pretend they don't want it when they do.* (Carnes, 2009, p 4)

These rationalisations distance the addict away from the true reality of his or her behaviour.

CHAPTER 11

# Predatory Flirting And Objectification

Among sex addicts seductive-role behaviour such as "predatory flirting" are common. Sex addicts use predatory flirting in order to seduce. Not all seductive-role sex addicts stop at the kiss, but all are merely interested in the seduction. Dr Patrick Carnes, ground breaking sex addiction expert and author of *Out of the shadows: Understanding sexual addiction* writes, "Seductive sex focuses on charming, persuading or manipulating others into sexual contact, and involves treating the other person as a conquest or a challenge, rather than someone else to connect with...". While the term may sound alarming, the "predatory" part does not indicate any illegal action. Regarding seductive-role sex addicts, predatory flirting refers to the way they seek out individuals solely for the purpose of fulfilling their need to experience the high of the chase. "Intriguing" is another word frequently used to refer to seductive-role sex addicts; in their case, it is used as a verb. Intriguing here is the act of romantic intrigue – the high that comes from seeking a romantic connection with another person. It is important to understand that for sex addicts, this connection is surface only, rather than deep or lasting. In seductive-role sex addiction, the addicts use another person as an object and enter an *object relationship* to make themselves feel more powerful and secure.

## *Object Relationship*

This includes fantasy, desire, obsession, disconnection. This cycle of objectifying women and/or men creates relational and societal issues, especially in someone living with sex addiction. The psychological consequences of objectification affect both the woman or man seen as the object and also the individual actively using people in their lives as sexual objects. This exploitation of other human beings as objects plays a large role in sexual addiction. Sex addicts feel a sense of release or freedom when engaging in their fantasy worlds. They tend to use the object of their obsession or their addictive sexual behaviours as a way to self-soothe, relax, escape, or experience validation.

Many people are faced with conflicting tension between sexuality and attachment needs. This tension causes the person to feel sexually attracted to someone without the need for a meaningful partnership; while the other side of the tension is when the same person feels strong separation anxiety in a long-lasting relationship where sexual attraction has already vanished.

## *Types of Objectification*

- **Denial of autonomy;** when the person/object is not allowed personal freedoms.

- **Fungibility;** when the person/object is easily replaceable with another similar person/object.

- **Inertness;** when the person/object is powerless and is allowed no control.

- **Instrumentality;** when the person/object's sole function is to be used as a device.

- **Ownership;** when the person/object is merely a possession and tangible commodity.

- **Denial of subjectivity;** when the person/object's emotions are not taken into consideration.

- **Violability;** when the person/object has no limits and boundaries are broken.

## *Object Relationship and Lack of Empathy and Intimacy*

Empathy is the ability to take into consideration another person's perspective without diluting this understanding by including your personal opinion or feelings. In the context of sex addiction, the sexual object is no longer viewed as an individual – someone with a personality, feelings or worth; instead, he or she is a source for sexual gratification. At the same time, the objectifier/sex addict develops a lack of intimacy and empathy due to the moral distraction of their sexual goals. Intimacy and empathy are neglected during objectification as true feelings and intentions are not shared to allow this bond to evolve past its sole purpose – sex. According to research, more than 87% of sex addicts come from a disengaged family environment in which family members are detached, uninvolved, or emotionally absent. Compulsive sexual behaviour is a sign of a significant intimacy disorder and the inability to meet emotional needs.

CHAPTER 12

# Common Personality Traits

Sex addicts commonly present with some similar personality traits, such as:

- Emotional insecurity
- Intolerance or frustration
- A tendency to action and to acting out
- A "belief" in an operative and mechanical sexual model
- The compulsive system
- Emotional overflow and self-destructive behaviours
- Difficulty with conjugal stability
- Rational anxiety

- Affective and social isolation
- Masked depression; and
- Defensiveness

## *Defensiveness and the Love/Sex Split*

Splitting is the essential defensive process employed by sex addicts. It aids in avoiding confrontation with the subject, in the face of his or her affective inconsistency, with depressive suffering. Splitting is the separation of affectionate impulses from sexual impulses. Although sex addicts do not invest quality time, thoughtfulness or emotional connection with their real partner, they are on the other hand investing in friends, family and out of reach partners. Denial feeds the splitting. Sex addicts can, with complete disregard, abandon a partner who has tenderly attached to them. Similarly, when a sex addict feels a sense of care towards a partner, reactions of distress or even violence may emerge. Sex addicts, through splitting, can display no apparent suffering during a major loss, separation or grieving process, for example.

## *Delusion*

Delusion refers to people's self-deceit and reliance on their own lies. You frequently observe sincere intentions in the addicts when making commitments to change, or follow through with what they have agreed on. Sex addicts may at times cry, express tenderness and a great deal of emotion – or even go into rage and anger if they feel their good intentions are not believed. Because of their severely impaired thinking, they may **"sincerely" be lying** and that is the reason their commitment to others is as empty as their self-promise to stop acting out.

## Common Personality Traits

Once again, this internal paradox may be difficult for a non-addicted individual to comprehend, but for a sex addict who is split and who carries the inner conflicts between the normal and the addict, this is a daily occurrence. Even the addicts are aware of being untrustworthy themselves, and do not trust others; thus, sex becomes their only trusted "friend" that they can count on. At least it will never fail to show up and relieve the distress and pain.

Sex addicts live with constant fear of judgment from others particularly if their compulsive sexual activities are exposed. Yet paradoxically, they place themselves in hazardous situations to get their fix, and the fear of discovery follows them like a shadow. Gradually, their fear turns into suspicion and paranoia that intensify the sense of isolation and alienation. The internal conflict, guilt and shame are heightened and the need to protect their secret life becomes a desperate necessity. As a result, they become skilled at blaming others for all the difficulties. Sex addicts learn to find faults in their partners, children, co-workers, etc. **Blaming others makes the sexual acting out/betrayal more justifiable.** In the addict's fabricated world, difficult partners, ungrateful children, work-related stress and unfair life circumstances warrant the King Baby (addict) to reach for his reward.

Although they are fearful of others' judgments, addicts themselves are judgmental, self-righteous and critical of others. Furthermore, their sense of entitlement is strong and they often act like **King Baby**. It is almost impossible to get a sex addict to accept personal responsibility for mistakes, shortcomings or behaviours. In other words, these behaviours isolate the addict's delusional world further from the real world and real people. The sexual addiction in the eyes of an addict is the source of nurturing and reliable care. To admit to one's faults or mistakes would ruin this illusion and taint their only dependable source (sex) for pain relief. The addict's patterns of **delusional thought** processes **denial, rationalisation, delusion, paranoia,** and **blame** prevents them from achieving an important avenue of self-knowledge and grasp of reality.

## *Addicted to External Validation*

Sex addicts lack self-confidence. They tend to fear being themselves, especially in social situations. They focus heavily on how others see them. Sex addicts tend to play roles. They don't have a strong sense of self, and instead, put on the appearance of playing someone else to receive external validation. Validation, in fact, is the human's need to know that having thoughts and emotions are accepted. Being validated is an innate need, it communicates understanding of ones' feelings, and gives the individuals reassurance that their feelings and thoughts are reasonable and okay. After all, humans are emotional beings and validation is fundamental to wellbeing. Through validation people relate and connect with each other and form wholesome relationships. However, the way a sex addict seeks validation is completely different. Their seeking is in a form of an external validation and not an internal (self-generated) validation. Instead, it is a requirement, a craving and an endless need. The sex addict's need for external validation is insatiable and has its roots in vanity, insecurity and low self-esteem.

This is the kind of validation where the sex addict does something and then expects – even needs – to be praised or verbally appreciated for it, otherwise self-esteem or self-worth takes a hit. Sex addicts before active recovery need external approval like a drug. They need compliments, to be told how great they are, and this is the only way for them to know that they are loved. In this way, it's really a false sense of confidence. Sex addicts before recovery are reliant on external validation and are often unable to confront people or disagree. Instead, they keep changing their thoughts and beliefs because someone else either approves or disapproves, and they keep ascribing their self-worth to the approval of others.

## *Examples of External Validations Include:*

(1) Social media validation. Engaging in social media has the potential to become addictive because it feeds this external validation tendency. Social media can condition the individual into someone who craves and needs others' approval, particularly from those who are not even too close with the individual.

(2) Social media as a means to receive external approval from women. Many male sex addicts become absolutely addicted to female attention and keep feeding their validation-seeking addiction through social media. Here, they have an avenue to be whoever they want to be, and continue living in a fabricated world while getting what they need – validation.

(3) Approval from external family and friends. Individuals get a hit of dopamine when they are told they did a good job or when they please someone who they consider to be superior or slightly above themselves in social standing. As these individuals get more and more validation, three things start to happen:

- It turns into a habit.
- The desire to receive more increases.
- Individuals will try to "one-up" themselves.

The desire for external validation can turn into a habit. A bad one. And fast. A habit that is formed by repetition. Repetition is encouraged once again by... dopamine.

## Idealization, and De-valorisation

Sex addicts commonly function with a black or white/ all or nothing mentality. They either idealize or de-valorise others. These both, image distorting and unconscious concepts are maladaptive defence mechanisms to protect the ego and ways of stress management. Idealization and de-valorisation are indications of the addict's inability during distress in providing an integrated view of a good and a bad in a person.

In psychological process idealization describes attributing overly positive qualities to another person or a thing. This is another way for the sex addict to cope with distress and anxiety. Here, an individual or an object of ambivalence is perceived as perfect or given exaggerated positive qualities.

> Estellon and Mouras (2012, p. 5) refer to idealisation and de-valorisation as:
>
> *The mechanism of idealization functions in a way that is complementary to splitting. A new person can be strongly idealised: presenting no failings, dotted with all possible qualities; they are apprehended as being "perfect". When the deceptions or frustrations have spoiled the perfection of this object, splitting allows the sex addict to depreciate them, to disdain them, and to stop investing in them immediately. De-valorisation is a corollary of omnipotence. It allows one, without suffering, to get rid of an object when it does not bring the expected or desired satisfaction. Splitting thus ensures that a part of the Ego remains idealised (the grandiose self) in such a way that the feelings of suffering, frustration, deception, desire, or hatred, when they are experienced, can always be imputed to the bad behaviour of others (blaming others). These exaggerated reactions permit the Ego – whose frontiers are unsure – not to collapse.*

**De-valorisation** or devaluation is a learned unconscious defence mechanism and contrary to idealization. It is applied when an individual considers themselves, an object, or others as completely imperfect, worthless, defective or as possessing exaggerated negative characteristics.

## *Relational Anxieties and Avoidance*

Sex addicts, from a relationship point of view, attempt to avoid real connections and encounters with others and use phobic strategies to achieve this. Once again, in this context sex addicts find themselves faced with paradoxes. They constantly carry the pressure of dealing with two different types of relationship tensions. On one hand they need to manage the anxiety of intrusion, and on the other hand they are faced with the anxiety of abandonment. **Preoccupation with these anxieties leads to unbearable attachment difficulties.** At times, these attachment uncertainties and constant internal conflicts make a relationship break up an easier choice.

In order for a sex addict to not lose their mind, he or she learns to "zap" from one body to another. Leaving one body, while zapping into another one, allows the anxiety of intrusion to be managed, and also the fear of abandonment. Zapping is a way for the addict to connect with fragments without worrying about the whole. Zapping operates through vision and fills the mind with images and feelings without allowing any time for real elaboration. Here, the sex addict experiences great impatience and wants nothing to do with delaying the relief. Switching bodies will allow the sex addict to dodge depressive distress associated with others' deceptions or others' attachment.

This explains why it is so scary for sex addicts to form true bonds with others; instead they learn to consume and use others as pleasure objects as a way to protect themselves. Although subconsciously a sex addict is hungry for love and attachment, in reality this notion is so fear-based that what is requested is only sex and sexual release. This sexual frenzy often covers up a strong and denied emotional deficiency.

## *Power and Control*

As mentioned earlier, a sex addict is faced by internal tensions of two co-existing needs. **One need is to avoid anxiety that true intimacy brings. The other is hunger and need for connection.** However, these paradoxes cannot co-exist and allow authentic relationship to thrive. Addiction, at least at first, deceitfully creates a sense of control, for the individual who is both desperate for safety through intimacy avoidance and desperate for true connection. Real human connection is difficult to define, it is elusive and experiential. Furthermore, true connection is transparent, while beyond will power or control. A sex addict's true self is concealed behind a veil of control and power. Vulnerability and reciprocation of power are required to form real connection. However, for sex addicts who mostly grew up within a hard shell of an "maladaptive" false self, vulnerability is terrifying and at times impossible to bear.

> *The false self, refers to certain types of false personalities that develop as the result of early and repeated environmental failure, with the result that the true self-potential is not realized, but hidden (Johns, para.1).*

Vulnerability is to expose oneself to potential re-traumatisation, betrayal, abandonment, enmeshment and desolation. For a sex addict it is safer (while self-defeating) to uphold control and power, particularly in performing sexual acts. There is less anxiety provoked when the sex addict controls the flavour of the act, writes the script, controls the participants and even pays them. Before recovery, due to their experiences of trauma and adapted faulty core beliefs, sex addicts are challenged by a lack of centeredness and an immature emotional IQ. The false self was created to safeguard the ego and ensure survival. Nevertheless, during recovery sex addicts learn that without vulnerability true intimacy is impossible.

## *Self-Destructive Behaviours*

Many sex addicts engage in high-risk behaviours, which may result in severe consequences, such as loss of career or even arrest. Children who are sexually abused often integrate fear into their arousal patterns. Later in life, it makes sense that for sex to work for these adults, it has to have a fear component, which results in risk-seeking sexual activities. Frequently, sex addicts report knowing their behaviour would be disastrous but engaged in it anyway.

## *Extreme Eroticisation and Shame*

One of the common occurrences observed in children growing up in abusive family systems or with trauma, is that as adults, these individuals tend to sexualise all interactions. These individuals also often feel that their relationship filters are different compared to others. Therefore, this adds to their sense of shame. Shame-based sense of self stems from a failure to achieve a positive sense of self and a profound belief in one's lack of worth. The constant inability to stop the behaviours and the past unresolved trauma/abuse confirm their belief that they are fundamentally flawed and unlovable.

## *Distrust of Authority*

According to research, most sex addicts come from dysfunctional families who have a significant problem with addictive and compulsive disorders. With less than 13% of the families of origin often reporting no addictions, or compulsive disorders presented in their family system. When children grow up in dysfunctional families, they can become overly rigid and controlling. Children from these families tend not to develop normal abilities of self-limitation and responsibility. Even, conforming with authority can mean a crucial loss of self for these individuals. As adults, these individuals learn to comfortably conceal things from authority figures and become extremely resistant to accountability.

## *Masters of Manipulation*

Sex addiction is all about manipulation, and sex addicts know how to manipulate to get their fix (sex). Being constantly manipulated by a partner is extremely distressing and can severely impact a person's physical and psychological wellbeing. It is heartbreaking to have suspicions about one's partner's activities confirmed, and that the suspicions were justified – the suspicious partner was not "crazy" or had mental issues. To uncover the tendency for manipulation one must pay attention to some telling signs. These may be displayed when:

- The individuals do not hold themselves accountable or take responsibility. This can occur by avoiding conversations, lying, acting innocent or playing the victim. On rare occasions when manipulators take responsibility, they make sure that their efforts are noticed while they subtly demand a return or acknowledgment. At times they may start asking for a bit of help, and it almost always becomes a "camel in the tent" situation.

- These individuals tend to make others feel guilty and blame them for their problems. When the situation arises that someone else makes a choice or raises a genuine complaint, the manipulators feel self-pity, play the victim and make the other person feel guilty. In other words, it is always another person's fault for every problem, and it is impossible to get a manipulator to take accountability.

- Manipulators lie compulsively and easily. Sex addicts learn early on to praise others and lie to release their share of work on others. They are great at twisting words and being deceitful to win an argument and to shift the blame from themselves on to others. Manipulators (sex addicts) make others doubt their own judgement, reality and sanity. This is commonly called the "gaslighting" method. Additionally, gaslighting includes feeding others (partners) lies, white lies and half-truths.

- Manipulators know how to undermine partners' self-confidence and self-esteem. They make their partners feel inadequate and small by implementing subtle criticism or through indirect berating remarks. The partners always feel they are walking on "eggshells" and whatever they do is not good enough. If a partner attempts to confront a sex addict (manipulator), he or she argues about supportive intentions. Once again, the complaining partner is left to doubt their reality and carry the blame.

- Sex addicts display manipulation through passive-aggressive behaviours. If their attempts in getting what they want has not been achieved through flattery, praising, emotional blackmail or constant nagging, they can start punishing the others through "silent treatment", "stone walling", "avoidance" or "withholding" what may be important to the other person.

- Sex addicts, through manipulation, may gradually and systematically isolate their partners from other close relationships. Some partners of sex addicts slowly lose their identity with their choices, plans and priorities always sacrificed while the sex addict takes the centre stage.

However, the positive news is that sex addicts can easily correct their manipulative behaviour once they enter active recovery, particularly when they seek therapy together with their intimate partners/family members.

## *Compartmentalisation*

Compartmentalisation is a survival mechanism for abused children to avoid a painful reality. However, for adults, it refers to distributing and dividing up life into various separated compartments. This explains how sex addicts may believe that nobody will ever discover their compulsive sexual behaviours, while they can easily lie to others without any distress.

Sex addicts can compartmentalise real life and real relationships while indulging in fantasies and sexual activities. It creates much tension, trying to hold two very different thoughts in the head at the same time. Compartmentalisation is a coping mechanism to deal with conflicting thoughts. When we compartmentalise, we can keep things separate to avoid all unpleasant feelings and thoughts.

## Common Personality Traits

Research has found that the majority of sex addicts love their partners, yet they act out without knowing *"why"*? Compartments act as "air-tight" containers that keep different and conflicting thoughts separate. This unhealthy process of compartmentalisation stems from:

- Psychological or physical neglect from primary caregivers/parents at an early age
- Violent parents/caregivers – out of control rage, experienced either directly or witnessed
- Childhood trauma, distressing memories or experiences that needed to be avoided by pushing them out of consciousness

When sex addicts compartmentalise, the following occurs:

- They prefer everything to have very definite beginnings/middles/endings.
- They are unable to, or have difficulties with, experiencing deep emotions and everything feels surface level.
- They experience a Dr Jekyll/Mr Hyde radical personality shift in different circumstances.
- People around them only know them superficially.
- They suffer from poor memory.

## *Gaslighting*

> Dr Robert Weiss (2015), describes this phenomenon as:
>
> *Gaslighting is a form of psychological abuse where false information is presented to the individual by a spouse or another primary attachment figure, causing the individual to doubt his or her perceptions, judgements, memories, and even sanity. Cleverly named after the 1944 Ingrid Bergman film, "Gaslight", gaslighting is a form of psychological control where one spouse manipulates the other into not trusting their perceptions of reality. (para.1).*

Sex addicts who gaslight behave like this to protect themselves and their secrets. The addict shifts blame and doubt onto their partner so emphatically that the partner starts to doubt their own perceptions. Most people believe that only sociopaths and psychopaths are using this type of manipulation, while most partners of sex addicts would have experienced this phenomenon to some extent in their relationship.

**Gaslighting in this sense of denying someone's intuitive sense of reality or making them believe they are crazy,** is a common type of manipulation and abuse.

When the partners of sex addicts have had their reality and intuitions contradicted for years and been told repeatedly that they are paranoid, unfair or controlling by their sex addict partner, gradually the betrayed partner feels that they are to blame for the problems and may suffer from emotional dysregulation. Over time, these partners are manipulated so much that they lose their faith in the ability to trust any perceived reality and consequently, blame themselves for their own thoughts and emotions. Gaslighting raises *the questioning of one's own reality.*

## Common Personality Traits

Therefore, in sex addiction recovery, couples need to address various injuries as a result of gaslighting behaviours and other damaging forms of manipulation.

CHAPTER 13

# Connection And Intimacy

It is well known that humans are relational beings and *hardwired* for intimacy and connectedness with others. Intimacy at times is referred to as *"in-to-me-see."* Real intimacy requires a deliberate attempt to allow the other person in and expose one's true self to them. Although, this may be a difficult task for most people, for sex addicts who carry a profound sense of worthlessness and shame, this is an unthinkable possibility. Sex addicts experience intimacy differently and it threatens them to exposure. Intimacy is terrifying and they will escape it at any cost. Sex addicts not only feel shame because of engaging in compulsive sexual acts but also from deep within themselves. The deep shame within has probably been there the longest and from the childhood. It has a loud voice about not only what they have done, but also who they are. Infants from the earliest moments seek out and require connection, attention and the affirmation of their caregivers. If they get what they need they will likely develop into seeking healthy relationships and intimacy in their later life.

Unfortunately, for many sex addicts, their earliest emotional needs were not met and their experiences prompted them into forming a distorted belief system about themselves. Beliefs such as "I am a bad person", "I am a failure", "surely if people knew the 'real me' they would not want anything to do with me", "people are not trustworthy" or "I am not lovable, otherwise my parents would love me" are often elements of their self-talk. This flawed belief system causes the sex addict to avoid intimacy and closeness at any cost because it would be unbearable if they would be seen as unworthy or unlovable by others. Intimacy becomes a scary notion and by avoiding it, they avoid rejection and pain.

The belief system of a non-addict individual allows coping with both acceptance and rejection by others. But for a sex addict with distorted core belief, reality gets inaccurate and consequently very scary. Sex addicts commonly struggle to have real close friendships or relationships. While many sex addicts get involved romantically, mostly have fear of true intimacy. It is the fear of failure as a human that keeps the sex addict from getting close to others. They consider each encounter as a test that involves being rejected or accepted as a worthy person. Sex addicts dislike going through this test, thus avoiding closeness provokes much less anxiety.

Sex addicts are also very hypervigilant individuals. They are **hypersensitive to criticism** or to the slightest hint that they are disliked. In this regard, they quickly interpret these experiences to verify their faulty core belief, that they are unworthy and not good enough. Sex addicts apply these core beliefs in two ways in relationships with others. One way is to act aloof and disengaged to protect against any possible rejection; or to become passive, pleasing and subservient to avoid distress or disapproval from others. Some sex addicts, depending on the situation and who they encounter, could switch between these roles. Intimacy avoidance causes the sex addict's authentic self, emotions, thoughts and attributes to be sacrificed and disregarded. After all, their belief is **that intimacy will lead to pain, and pain must be avoided no matter what the payoff**. In reality the payoff for a sex addict is the disconnection and loneliness from self and others.

Sex addicts' fear of intimacy causes **self-sabotage**, which is another sign of their intimacy disorder. On the one hand, they display intimacy avoidance while on the other hand, they experience extreme fear of abandonment. This phenomenon could sometimes be regarded as a genuine personality disorder. The fear of abandonment by a loved one or feeling of loneliness is a psychological experience and often has its root and triggers in past events. Fear of abandonment includes losing parents, absent caregivers, a loved one's death, and/or rejection by a romantic partner. This type of fear is due to an incomplete grieving process where the person has not resolved their grief. These fears must be processed and dealt with so the person can form healthy platonic or romantic relationships.

To reiterate our discussion: sex addiction is a coping mechanism, and a way to avoid intimacy and real human connection. Many sex addicts were physically, emotionally or sexually abused as children and that abuse eroded their ability to trust. Driven by fear of rejection and fear of abandonment, sex addicts, usually in childhood, were profoundly rejected or abandoned. Perhaps this was in the early years or even adulthood, but the feelings of abandonment or rejection were so severe that they left emotional scars. As a result, they find it extremely difficult to sustain lasting intimacy or healthy relationships. Through addiction, sex addicts avoid deep emotional pain. Although **physical intimacy may be easy for sex addicts, emotional intimacy is virtually impossible because emotional intimacy requires trust, vulnerability, transparency and openness.**

## *Intimacy Anorexia*

Over 30% of individuals with sex addiction have intimacy anorexia. According to Dr Weiss (2020, para.1):

*Intimacy anorexia is a relationship disorder that is marked by a lack of intimacy in a relationship. It occurs when someone in a relationship actively withholds emotional, spiritual and sexual intimacy from their spouse or partner. This lack of intimacy harms the marriage, damages the relationship causing pain and loneliness and impacts the spouse or partner significantly.*

- Withholding love
- Withholding praise or open appreciation of partners
- Unable to express or share true feelings or take criticism
- Controlling through silence and anger or money
- Blaming the partner
- Withholding sex or spiritual connection
- Attempting to stay busy to avoid time spent with the partner
- Treating their partner like a roommate

The sex addict's double bind (needing sex for relief of guilty behaviour, so indulging in more guilty behaviour) contains extreme tension that causes a vicious cycle that can only be broken through professional therapy and the path to a committed recovery. In this torturous double bind, the addict desires connection but is missing psychic or emotional fortitudes to achieve that. In this context, strength is lacking and genuine relationships require strength – and strength cannot flourish without a genuine relationship. Therefore, the addict's inner voice commands them to preserve the false, masked self. The prospect of real connection and intimacy gets left behind as an illusion. This is a painful realisation that drives the individual to more unhealthy behaviours while eroding all hope of actualisation and real human connectedness.

> **There is a tension created when a person both craves and fears true intimacy – that can only come through successfully encountering vulnerability which the person dealing with sex addiction cannot experience until during and after active therapy and recovery.**

# CHAPTER 14

# Co-occurring Conditions

Sex addiction rarely occurs in isolation and is commonly co-occurring with other disorders. In his book *Out of the shadows: Understanding sexual addiction* Dr Patrick Carnes observed that:

> *Research has found that 38% of sex addicts also struggle with an **eating disorder**. By far, the most common combination of addictions is when the sexual addict is also dependent on **alcohol** or another **drug**. Many people attribute sexual excesses and even incest to the power of alcoholism. The reality is that alcoholism often is a concurrent illness with, rather than the cause of, the sexual addiction. Many alcoholics have discovered that the treatment of one addiction does not cure the other. Thus, they need to seek recovery for each separately. Further,*

*many discover that they drink or use drugs to obliterate the pain of their sexual behaviour. There is growing documentation about the interaction between the two addictions.* (Carnes, 2009, p 9).

Carnes further reported that:

*Forty-two per cent of sex addicts have a problem with **substance/chemical** dependency. Among cocaine addicts, 50% to 70% have a problem with sexual compulsion. Other co-occurring conditions such as **shoplifting, gambling** and **spending** are frequent counterparts. **Physical violence** as a way to release pent-up tension is often reported as concurrent behaviour by sexually abusive families. The **workaholic** who gets high on the excitement of a new achievement finds professional life even more exhilarating when coupled with sexual addiction. In that case, the sexual and work addict marries the job. **Emotional illness** also flourishes within the addict's world. **Depression, bipolar disorders, suicide, obsessive-compulsive behaviour,** and **post-traumatic stress disorder** are frequent companions to the addiction.* (Carnes, 2009, p 9).

Sex addicts commonly carry **masked depression** which often constitutes the backdrop upon which sexually addictive behaviour is formed. Current research links the recourse to sexual addictions and elements of narcissistic depression, such as the loss of self-esteem. The loss of belief in the positive effects of a relationship, the loss of hope in others, progressively makes one lose sight of the meaning of a life that has – despite the erotic sensations that exhaust themselves in compulsive repetition – become sad and empty.

Many addicts seek treatment for these mental illnesses, while concomitant sexual addiction is ignored. Yet the sexual addiction

## Co-occurring Conditions

compounds the mental health issues. By far, and according to research, the most devastating emotional risk is suicide. 17% of sex addicts have attempted suicide, while 72% have thought of it.

Usually, compulsive sexual behaviour is part of an intricate wave of behaviours to manage internal distress. Some studies have shown a close connection between cocaine use and sexual acting out. Various reports also document switching or replacing one set of addictive/compulsive behaviours with another set. Concomitant mental health disorders include other **mood disorders, anxiety disorders, and abnormal personality traits,** all of which complicate treatment planning.

CHAPTER 15

# Recovery

**Sex addiction is a multifaceted condition, and successful recovery requires a holistic approach.** Thus, multiple modalities must be applied in order to cover each aspect of the condition. Treatment for sex addiction includes a combination of individual and couple therapy, psychotherapy (including group and family therapy), trauma processing, EMDR (eye movement desensitisation reprocessing), 12-step groups, neurofeedback, and in some cases, medication. For some, residential treatment programs, which provide intensive treatment in a structured setting, are available and can be very beneficial. However, since shame is a huge factor with sex addicts, many never seek treatment or resist the suggestion of it.

In a study in the early 90s Patrick Carnes followed 1,000 families for seven years, sex addicts and their partners, and published his results in a book called, *Don't call it love: Recovery from sexual addiction.* He discovered a very useful pattern for recovery.

Carnes found **individuals who made a successful recovery were the ones who early on in recovery had an educated and well-trusted therapist that they saw for about three to five years.** Carnes believes that in order to achieve changes in the brain, one of the first things individuals have to feel is safety; and, so, it must be a therapist that they really trust. It must also be somebody who can hold the individual very accountable. It is very important to have that accountability, where the therapist functions as a primary contractor, who sends the sex addict out to get various things and oversees the whole process over time. **Past unresolved trauma and abuse, maladaptive thought and behavioural patterns need to be explored and processed.** Sex addiction is about escapism of negative emotions; therapy can teach them how to sit with their emotions – instead of escaping or medicating them.

According to Carnes, the second thing that is really important is that addicts must be in a psychotherapy group which increases their ability to attach in healthy ways.

The third thing Carnes emphasises is participation in 12-step meetings.

Addicts must establish roots in a caring community. Like psychotherapy groups, with the support of 12-step meetings, *"addicts can stay straight as they struggle for a perspective on their lives. With help, addicts can integrate new beliefs and discard dysfunctional thinking. All forms of addiction are vicious because they deepen the inability to trust others. Yet without help from others, the addict cannot regain control because the addiction feeds itself. Sexual addiction is especially virulent because few forms of fixation or excitement are as supercharged with social judgement, ridicule, or fear. Consequently, seeking help is especially difficult for the sexual addict"* (Smith, 2019, pp. 4-5).

Thus a 12-step program can help members restore the living network of human relationships, especially in the family.

The fourth thing that Carnes found effective in recovery was for the addict to actually **do the step work**. Often, sex addicts are rushing to complete their steps without actually learning to live the steps. Some sex addicts even believe that there is a benefit to completing the 12-steps in 12 days or less. This mindset is concerning because these individuals need the time to absorb and process each step and apply them in their day to day life. Interactions with family, friends and others require a deep understanding and application of the 12 steps in all aspects of life to form new and authentic relationships. Others believe by attending numerous meetings and keeping themselves busy they are going through recovery, which is far from the truth. Active recovery requires actively doing the required work.

According to Carnes, therapists must monitor and help with the steps too, because if a sex addict, for example, takes step four and five, which basically are concerned with an emotional and moral education, the therapist needs to be intimately involved as this is literally how the sex addict starts to get their conscience back. Regaining their moral compass and their ability to tolerate negative emotions are major thresholds in recovery that has to happen. The therapist needs to be very involved with this step work.

The fifth thing that Carnes found that was very **important in active recovery was simply involving the partner and family in**

**the process**. Carnes warns against providing individual therapy only for the addict, as sex addiction concerns the whole family and the partner/family must also participate in therapy. Carnes continues to say if the sex addict only seeks individual therapy, they often make things worse. Couples therapy and family therapy, as well as individual therapy and group therapy are key to recovery. This entails a significant commitment. Carnes refers to the three-legged stool…**my recovery, your recovery, our recovery.** He says that the very worst thing that can happen is when the spouse is seeing one therapist in one office, and the addict is seeing another therapist in another office. It is so destructive, especially if the partner's wife does not understand addiction or the implications of addiction or how the brain has been impacted. If they have no concept of that, then they see this essentially as a matter of betrayal. If they are not on the same page with the treating therapist, that's a disaster. Thus, Carnes recommends that it is best to keep them in the same practice.

The sixth thing significant in recovery is **spirituality**. Some therapists like to think it is all related to their professional skills, but when individuals following recovery are asked to describe all the things that helped them to get well, they talk about spiritual life. This is not whether you are Jewish or Christian, or Buddhist, it makes no difference, but the recovering sex addicts really need to get in touch with their own spirituality and connect to a higher power, whatever or whoever their higher power is. Most sex addicts have a hard time being by themselves.

They need to engage in something to stimulate themselves. The whole notion of the deep stillness they need to experience in order to come to terms with what is really happening with themselves is foreign. They don't have a connection with themselves. If they cannot connect with themselves, they cannot connect with others;

if they cannot connect with others, then they cannot connect with a higher power or God. Spiritual life, as Henri Nouwen said, is the ability to be with yourself, and is key to "converting loneliness into solitude".

The seventh pillar of recovery is **resilience and gratitude**, which is a part of spirituality. The core of recovery is resilience, and resilience comes from taking that which is bad and negative and making it into something powerful and meaningful in life. Developing resilience skills, like gratitude, involve writing gratitude lists regularly, learning how to reframe negative perceptions into positive ones, learning the serenity prayer, practising letting go. In other words, a lot of this recovery has to do with the ability to take the ugliness of life and to learn from it, and to start listening to the inner observer in the brain that psychologically detaches itself and then monitors the traffic of the brain.

The eighth important concept in recovery is structure and **discipline**. As you start to grow and you have a structure to be able to change yourself, and you start to build trust for yourself, all your relationships shift – they deepen and become more meaningful.

The final thing that Carnes found that can really make a difference in recovery is **personal, emotional and physical health care**. Studies found that individuals who exercise, eat well, meditate, practise mindfulness and who journaled their emotions and thoughts did better. Now we know that all those things that help the heart, also help the brain. One of the things that sex addicts have to learn about is regarding their body, how their arousal works, how the neuropathways of the brain work; but they also need to become good consumers of health information about the brain. They need to learn about the brain's plasticity. They need to learn about mechanisms of attention that they need to cultivate; to concentrate their focus, and be able to really retrain their brain so that it becomes easier to the point of recovery from their addiction.

## *Mindfulness, Meditation and Relapse Prevention and Brain Mechanisms*

In the treatment of addiction, particularly sex addiction and dealing with cravings and urges, mindfulness-based practices have become increasingly mainstream and accepted.

The "*being*" mode of mindfulness is a state in which the individual can experience a trigger and the resulting temptation without allowing it to become all-consuming in their mind. It brings the ability to take a step back.

Mindfulness may improve the functioning of the reward system. It enhances drive, motivation and emotional processing and calms the disruptions in the inhibition of behaviour and self-monitoring functions. Studies on mindfulness meditation found that there was decreased "*activation of the amygdala (part of the pleasure circuitry) in response to emotional stimuli during mindfulness/meditation practice, carried over even at a later time*". (Hatch, 2019, para. 12)

The essential element of mindfulness practice is learning to let go. "*This means letting go of judging, comparing, competing, and trying to control things (including oneself). Whether this is experienced as giving over control to a "higher power", God or to the universe, or just letting go pure and simple, the result is likely the same. The practice makes available a state of stillness, serenity and acceptance which appears to allow the addicted brain to recover*". (ibid, final para)

There seem to be two factors at play in the addict's relapse. One is the lack of self-awareness during negative emotional states which may lead to relapse, and the other is over-reactivity to external cues signalling the addictive object. **Mindfulness practice and meditation appear to help in increasing self-awareness and decreasing reactivity when combined with therapy.** Meditation commonly describes an inward-turned state of consciousness while staying quiet and letting go of any thoughts or feelings. When thoughts or emotions come, they are not judged or entertained, but allowed to pass and move on. Combination of the two notions is referred to as "mindfulness/meditation." Both mindfulness and meditation have been found to enhance addiction recovery. Meditation has long been shown to ease muscle tension, reduces the activity of the sympathetic branch of the nervous system, and decreases heart rate and blood pressure.

## *Practising Mindfulness*

Sit comfortably and practise breathing deeply, feeling what the air feels like as it flows in and out of your body. As you do this for three minutes you will become more relaxed. If your mind wanders onto something else, just notice it and bring it back to your breath.

After three minutes, allow your thoughts, feelings, sensations to come and go, let them pass by your mind's eye without judging them. You will become more aware and able to see what is contributing to, defining, creating, expanding, contracting or somehow else impacting your life. The brain is kind of like a dinner buffet. Your brain gets to decide what gets served up every day, but as consumers, you get to choose what you eat by giving your attention to it. If you stop giving your attention to the unappetising stuff in your mental dinner buffet, the brain will stop being so eager about serving it up.

Mindfulness helps in developing the ability to **see thoughts in a more objective way**. It means instead of just being whisked away by habitual thought patterns; you get to decide if you want to take the ride. Mindfulness is never about stopping the thoughts, but about **changing the relationship with thoughts** so there can be more choice in what you consume. Prayer, meditation, or mindfulness are coping skills that can help replace negative behaviours. They also help you to accept things as they are, at that moment. Take time to be still and quiet in a busy world filled with commotion, and you'll find that the path becomes easier. It is a path towards the real inner comfort the individual once hoped he or she would find through sex addiction. One way to practice mindfulness is to learn "urge surfing".

## *Urge Surfing*

Whenever you feel an urge or craving you basically only have two choices:

To act upon it, or not to act upon it.

In this regard, ask yourself: "If I act on this urge, will I be acting like the ideal person I want to be? Will it help me take my life in the direction I want to go?" or "Would this action drives me further from my goals and values"?

If the answer is yes, then it makes sense for you to act on that urge. For example, if you have worked all day without a break and have the urge to rest.

On the other hand, don't if you have the urge to act out sexually. And if this urge is not in alignment with who you want to be, then it's best not to act on it.

## Recovery

Remember, when you are triggered your sex addiction patterns are activated and the more you give in, the stronger you reinforce these patterns.

Triggers could be: hunger, loneliness, emotional or physical tiredness, being angry or resentful or stressed.

The thoughts and automatic beliefs that cause you to sexually act out have been given priority in your mind and run by your unconscious mind. At that point you run on automatic pilot, and are essentially controlled by them. Bring them into consciousness. You are responsible for taking control of them. You are responsible to get well.

Acting on automatic pilot and according to the old patterns are fundamentally mindlessness and fusion. You lose your presence and fuse with your pornified and automatic thoughts. However, there is a solution to this problem. It is practising **mindfulness**.

To control your urges effectively do the following:

1. Notice them, become aware of them and acknowledge them.
2. Tell yourself silently "I am having the urges to do "X" or "to act out".
3. Check your values, and ask "Would acting out move me towards or away from my values and the person I desire to become"?
4. Ask "What happened all those times that I gave in? Did I feel better or did I only intensify and delay the pain?"

According to your honest answers, feel free to act out or stop. However, if the answer is to avoid acting out then take actions that are more aligned with your values.

Stop resisting the urges as you only increase your struggles. Stay open to your urges and know that they will subside and leave if you avoid suppressing or escaping them. Urge surfing is like wave surfing.

Have you ever watched ocean waves? A wave starts off small and gently grows. Then it slowly increases in speed and in size. Then it expands until it reaches its maximum size. However, once it has reached its peak, it slowly becomes smaller and smaller. The same happens with sexual urges in your body. Your urges start off small and then slowly increase in size. When you give an ocean wave enough space, it will reach its peak and then gradually diminish. On the other hand when a wave encounters resistance, such as crashing onto a beach or slam against rocks, it gives a loud noise, and can become destructive.

In sexual urge surfing avoid resisting the urge waves that happen in your head. Instead simply surf on them until they diminish on their own and you feel they do not have control over you.

**Do this:**

First, **watch**, acknowledge and just notice your bodily sensations.

Then you **accept** the feeling and silently say "I'm having sexual urges".

Pay attention to your **breathing** and give yourself permission to stay open and make room for what you are experiencing.

**Rate your urges from scale 0 to 10.** For example: "I have the urge to watch porn or masturbate and it is a 7". This will externalise the urges and allow you to defuse from the thoughts.

**Stay present** with your urges and bodily sensations. Become an observer and observe your own ocean waves without acting on them. Remember the waves, no matter how high they get, will gradually dissipate if you allow enough space instead of resisting them.

**Re-align** yourself with your values. Say out loud: "No" to acting out.

"I choose to know that I am sober".

"I choose to know that I am moving towards my values and the person I deserve to be".

**Do opposite actions.** Ask yourself "what actions can I take to enhance my life and values in the long term instead of resisting or controlling my urges"?

In summary, to manage your sexual urges effectively, you need to ACT:

A = Accept your thoughts and feelings.

C = Connect with your values.

T = Take effective action.

Urge surfing is an effective tool, and like any tool it needs ongoing practice. Journaling and sitting in your emotions before and during urge surfing will help you master this skill. Ongoing urge surfing practices on unrelated urges can increase your ability and effectiveness, enough to face even your strongest sexual urges. This technique is also a great idea for any other urges that comes up; the urge to drink, gamble, eat chocolate, the urge to overeat, etc.

## *Spiritual Growth and Recovery*

One of the essential pillars of effective recovery is spiritual growth.

Spiritual growth defines a connection to self, others, the world, and to a higher purpose (higher power) than oneself. It may involve representation of values such as trust, faith, respect, self-expression and hope.

Religion and/or spirituality can play an important role in recovery from addiction for some people, here are the reasons why:

### *1. Gives a sense of purpose*
Finding one's sense of purpose has shown to be a crucial aspect of effective recovery. Several current studies have found that when a person has a greater focus on purpose in life, that purpose has a profound positive impact on addiction recovery outcomes. For some individuals during recovery connection to God or a higher power brings a sense of purpose, and offers them the benefit of belonging to something more powerful than themselves.

### *2. Feels like one is making a contribution*
Research has shown us that giving to others actually makes us feel better. Helping other people as a way to help oneself is what drives many people through to beating their addiction. Sponsorship in a 12-step program, mentorship, or volunteering in a homeless shelter are some examples.

### *3. Brings mindfulness to recovery*
Living in the present moment and focusing on the now, not the future or the past, helps to centre and focus thoughts while reducing stress and anxiety. Focusing on the past triggers depression and

focusing on the future and "what ifs" leads to anxiety. Both are out of reach; the present moment is all there is.

### 4. Connects one to something greater than self
It brings an isolated person back to the revelation that they are not alone, even when they are by themselves, is a spiritual idea that helps many people in dealing with their addiction. Many people isolate and disconnect when they engage in their addictive behaviour, and that isolation can drive them further into their addiction. For those that do not believe in a God, per se, finding something greater is still attainable as long as they are open-minded, meditate or pray, help people, and keep searching for something bigger than themselves to believe in. The knowledge that there is a higher authority or power that exists even in solitude can have a profound psychological impact on an individual's overall wellbeing.

### 5. Establishes the person as part of a community
Addiction is isolating and lonely – it causes isolation due to bad behaviour, dishonesty, and shame. Working to become a part of a community of people who are going about their daily lives and interacting with them is a significant step in getting one's life back on track. Starting to connect with a community and building relationships with self and others are some of the beginning steps of recovery.

### 6. Teaches the practice of gratitude
Being grateful for things you value in life and focusing on them brings positivity into the soul. Beyond feeling positive emotions, practising gratitude is associated with physical muscle relaxation too. Gratitude practice can have a positive influence on overall physical and psychological wellbeing. Those who practise being grateful tend to be less depressed and have a higher level of belonging in the external world.

### 7. Provides accountability

Taking responsibility and being accountable for one's actions to the higher authority assists the individual to remain steadfast and have a greater sense of purposefulness. Furthermore, during the recovery process, staying accountable leads the person towards more productivity in society. To achieve genuine accountability, one must remain honest with one's self and others, and practise reflection and mindfulness on an ongoing basis to develop self-awareness and authenticity.

## EMDR (Eye Movement Desensitization Reprocessing)

Gabor Mate, MD who is an expert in addiction asks: *"Don't ask why the addiction, ask why the pain?"* (Vancouver EMDR Therapy, 2019, para. 3)

> Robert Miller (2011, p. 1) a lead researcher says that:
>
> *When positive feelings become rigidly linked with specific objects or behaviour, this linkage between feeling and behaviour, is called a feeling-state. When the feeling-state is triggered, the entire psycho-physiological pattern is activated. The activation of the pattern then triggers the out-of-control behaviour.*

Therefore, getting to the root cause of the pain for men and women experiencing sexual addiction often means addressing underlying trauma. Research consistently shows the frequency of emotional, physical, and sexual abuse in this group which can cause post-traumatic stress disorder (PTSD). Eye movement desensitization and reprocessing (EMDR) has become a leading method of intervention with trauma and PTSD with effective results in an extremely short time.

The word trauma comes from the Greek term meaning "to wound." Sometimes "talk therapy" is not enough to heal the wound. EMDR therapy works directly with the brain, and the way memories, thoughts, feelings and body sensations are stored when people are traumatised.

EMDR therapy has been found to be very effective as a comprehensive therapy approach when included in a recovery plan from sexual addiction. EMDR is not only reserved for the sex addicts – others can benefit from this treatment modality. Partners who have been deeply impacted and at times traumatised by their sex addict partner can benefit from EMDR treatment. In the aftermath of discovery or disclosure of sex addiction, the intimate partners often experience trauma responses. These responses include: rage, shock, intrusive images and thoughts, depression, low self-esteem, self-blame, feelings of betrayal, sense of lack of safety, feeling abandoned, nightmares, panic attacks and more. Most therapy programs including 12-step programs do not address the sex addict's trauma or partners' betrayal trauma. EMDR reaches the root cause of trauma; for the best long-lasting results it is to be used in combination with other treatment modalities.

**Whether the couples decide to stay in their relationship or separate, it is crucial that they both seek proper therapy. If they intend to stay together, the best treatment outcome is for them both to enter therapy with the same therapist, and have individual and couple's therapy on an ongoing basis.**

## *EDMR for sex addicts*

- EMDR during addiction recovery has its foundation on the essential principles of human behaviour. According to basic human behaviour, individuals move away from pain and move towards pleasure. In other words, if a behaviour or act brings about a negative consequence, then there has to be a positive feeling attached to it for the person to continue repeating it.

- Sex addiction is known as a behavioural addiction. The true desire is for the emotions that motivate sexual behaviour and not the behaviour itself. It is an escape from pain, seeking pleasure as a relief. EMDR can enhance positive feelings such as being lovable, worthy, good enough, in control and important through de-linking the positive emotional state.

- The root cause of sex addiction is mostly trauma (89%). EMDR can reach to the source (trauma) safely and effectively. Unresolved trauma will drive the sexual behaviours to feed a positive emotional state and escape the distress. EMDR therapy can assist in processing the past or present traumatic experiences.

- Many sex addicts have had attachment wounds in their childhood. These attachment injuries in adulthood cause the sex addict to struggle with intimacy and relationship building. EMDR can assist in healing childhood attachment wounds and heal from them safely.

As mentioned earlier EMDR is also valuable for the partner of sex addicts who experience a wide range of symptoms and negative emotions in the aftermath of exposure to their partner's compulsive sexual activities.

## *EMDR for partners of sex addicts*

- EMDR therapy can assist the partners by targeting the unpleasant memories that cause them distress. Exposure to a partner's compulsive sexual behaviours commonly causes betrayal trauma which has severe physical and psychological impacts. EMDR can aid in relief from trauma responses such as nightmares, anxiety or other emotional distress.

- Many partners of sex addicts form negative self-beliefs about themselves because of the betrayal. Research has found lower self-esteem, self-blame and feelings of failure and worthlessness are some of the common thoughts and beliefs that partners adopt in the aftermath of exposure to their partner's sex addiction. EMDR can help heal this negative self-talk and beliefs. EMDR processes the troubling memories connected to these faulty beliefs and transform them to more helpful and positive beliefs (e.g., I did my best, I am worthy, I am not to blame, I am lovable).

- Dealing with the aftermath of sex addiction-induced betrayal trauma can be overwhelming and daunting. EMDR enhances the relational strength and assists couples living a fuller life. Trauma must be dealt with in a safe and effective way and once the symptoms have reduced, the couples can decide to stay together or separate. EMDR can bring clarity in decision making as it reduces the trauma responses.

Dr. Fai Seyed Aghamiri

## *NeurOptimal® Neurofeedback*

Neurofeedback is an information technology that offers training to the brain, giving it the opportunity to function at its best. In this way NeurOptimal® Neurofeedback functions as a unique dynamical system. It regulates the nervous system and as a result offers a brain-body connection to overall wellness. It is a mathematically designed system to communicate directly with the central nervous system. The internal brain communication occurs via electrical impulses called brain waves. Neurofeedback is a computerised system that communicates directly to the brain. This communication is as if a mirror is held up to the brain, enabling it to see and correct itself. Every time the brain is provided with this information, it makes essential alterations by what is called neural plasticity (which is the ability of the nervous system to adapt, grow and change). Similar to EMDR, NeurOptimal® Neurofeedback is best to be used within a holistic approach that is joined with lifestyle changes and psychotherapy. As the brain begins to change (neural plasticity), Neurofeedback results are further enhanced when individuals employ healthy lifestyle choices, healthy nutrition, mindfulness and meditation, and other body-based behaviours to elevate their overall wellness. Neurofeedback can help clients balance and normalise their brain function and body regulation.

NeurOptimal® Neurofeedback is not a treatment but a therapy that can be helpful with:

- Addictions
- ADHD/ADD
- Anxiety
- Post-traumatic stress disorder (PTSD)
- Obsessive-compulsive disorder (OCD)
- Sleep issues

## Recovery

- Traumatic brain injury (TBI) and concussions
- Mood issues
- Anger/explosiveness
- Chronic headaches/migraines
- Chronic stress
- Cognition and clarity
- Performance optimisation

A combination of Neurofeedback and EMDR therapy can lead to a better treatment outcome.

# CHAPTER 16

# Compassion Vs Condemnation

You may ask why sex addicts deserve our compassion? After all, they have made poor choices with devastating consequences for everyone involved. The answer is, would we not feel compassion for heroin addicts who are injecting themselves with infected needles, not knowing whether what they shoot up is actual heroin or not?

Would drug addicts, alcoholics or gambling addicts have any capacity to grasp the true impact of their actions? Not until during and after recovery. This is the same with sex addiction. Sex addiction is like another addiction, a brain disease.

Sex addiction is not really about sex or liking sex too much. Like food addiction, it is not actually about the cakes and biscuits. It is all about escaping intolerable feelings, the past trauma, the negative messages and shame that were received growing up. Sex addiction is like "the black sheep of the family" in the family of addictions. When there is a dependency on alcohol or drugs, total abstinence is essential for recovery. But, unfortunately, when sex is the addiction, it is often looked at as a "moral failing" which brings forth shame in the addict. In truth, although sex addiction is no different to dependency on alcohol, drugs, food or gambling, usually it has more shame and stigma for the individual and their family. Dr Patrick Carnes, in his book *A Gentle Path Through the Twelve Steps*, offers these facts about addiction generally, and sex addiction specifically:

- *All addictions, even if they do not involve alcohol or other drugs, impact the same centres of the brain.*
- *Addiction changes the brain, laying down neural networks that chemically encourage us to repeat harmful, compulsive behaviours.*
- *Addictions are interactive. One addiction can trigger, replace or heighten another through a measurable biochemical process in the brain.*
- *Whether it's slugging back a litre of vodka, snorting an eight ball of cocaine up your nose, binging on chips and ice cream or having sex with multiple partners a day, these are just the symptoms. The effects on our brains, the consequences and underlying causes are the commonalities we should focus on.*

Addiction is addiction is addiction. Sex addiction is not different to any other substance addiction or gambling addiction. Therefore, sex addicts deserve the same compassion and treatment as those with dependencies on alcohol, drugs or gambling. Many sex addicts carry heavy guilt and shame around. One of the hardest parts of sobriety is having to confront unpleasant emotions without recourse to compulsive sexual behaviours.

This is often how addiction begins in the first place. When the individual's feelings, thoughts, and memories are persistent and painful, any kind of relief is welcome. Not knowing how to deal with negative feelings can be difficult, and often leads to relapse. Guilt can be a useful emotion when it prompts the person to do the right thing, while false guilt and shame give the message that the offending person is bad, unworthy and a failure.

False guilt is driven by the unconscious mind and is an effective tool to keep the person in the deprivation loop. It is a response learned at an early age and triggered by an external need that could not be met. False guilt is unreasonable; it is guilt applied incorrectly and always leads to self-sabotage. A person who carries false guilt will get stuck in a cycle of negative thoughts, emotional pain and self-judgement. False guilt prevents the individual from intimacy with others, and fearful of success. Increased defensiveness, feeling judged by others, and even paranoia at times are other by-products of false guilt. It is a form of self-abuse and undermines the true self. Self-sabotage keeps the FEAR (False Evidence Appearing Real) and deprivation alive.

Shame says "surely if people knew the 'real me' they would not want to be with me". In reality, carrying false guilt and shame are both counterproductive to recovery. Obsessing about being a failure, unworthy and unable to change past mistakes is a sure way to stay in the negative mindset of self-loathing. If individuals insist on staying in deep shame and feeling miserable, they are likely to have a hard time with sobriety and relapse is imminent.

Carrying false guilt and shame also isolates and disconnects the person from self and others. Feeling like you are a rotten person who does not deserve forgiveness or compassion makes it very hard to connect with people, or open up to anyone. When individuals blame themselves for their mistakes, this can lead to self-destructive and self-sabotaging behaviour. The challenges faced by addicts are magnified because our society stigmatises addicted individuals who may feel judged. In other words, sex addicts can feel that they are deserving of carrying shame or judgement.

False guilt, shame, low self-esteem, anger, fear, anxiety, rejection and despair are some of the many negative emotions that must be dealt with during recovery and the very important process of learning self-forgiveness. Lack of self-forgiveness can stimulate many negative feelings. These may include sadness, loneliness, unworthiness, fear, guilt, grief, shame, and remorse. Carrying these feelings can disrupt recovery or directly lead to relapse. When a person's anger is targeted towards one's self because of past reckless behaviour, the individual often ends up lashing out at someone else. This will once again escalate self-hatred and fuel more rage and anger. If the person is stuck in the cycle of shame as a result, then self-confidence will decrease which triggers relapse. Many sex addicts struggle with the concept of forgiveness to oneself or others. However, forgiveness is always valuable however challenging it may seem. Journaling and sharing thoughts and feelings in therapy are essential steps towards achieving forgiveness.

Here are some suggestions for self-forgiveness during recovery:

### *Radical acceptance*
It means admitting that mistakes have been made, and accepting that what has been done is done, it cannot be undone but it will not be repeated. It also means acknowledging the emotions of guilt

and shame without acting upon them. Acceptance is a vital part of recovery. It means coming to terms with ourselves and our lives – the essence of acceptance – and without this, there will be struggles to find true serenity or inner peace. Dwelling on mistakes is pointless unless one learns from them and resolves to do better in future. Accepting one's mistakes will allow the addict to move forward.

### *Identification and learning*
Taking the time to identify, examine, and learn from the situations that are challenging are essential during effective recovery. It is not only about *what* was done; it is about *why* it was done. While addiction may have influenced the person to act poorly, it is essential to identify the underlying, cause, attitude or belief, rather than the addiction itself, that prompted the behaviour.

Analysing the feelings that led to compulsive behaviours will assist to put the situation into a rational perspective, making the self-forgiveness concept easier to accept.

### *Shared experiences, strength and hope*
Active listening and speaking to others are some of the best actions to take during recovery. Honest sharing of thoughts and feelings will lead to encouragement and may also help in getting much-needed hope and feedback from others who have been in the same situation. This can also make the person less lonely in their struggles and closer to self-forgiveness.

### *Remorse and making up for past mistakes*
For the sex addict, often expressing a verbal apology to a partner /others is not enough – or even not accepted. This can hurt the self-esteem. For this reason, addicts in early recovery must be cautious to think carefully before trying to make amends by verbal apologies only. Instead, demonstrate remorse and amendment

through behaviours and actions. Consistency, serving others or the community, and persistence in displaying healthy behaviours are indications of active recovery.

### *Your recovery is ongoing – take it seriously*

The recovery process needs you to be vigilant, and to take a serious approach in order to implement it. Recovery does not only mean abstinence from compulsive sexual activities. Recovery means you recover both in your sexual compulsivity and in your relationships. Healthy relationships that have clear boundaries, empathy for self and others, avoiding defensiveness, honesty, accountability and working and living the recovery steps (instead of only doing them) are all part of a holistic recovery program. Sex addiction is about dysfunctional relationships with self and others. Therefore, recovery from sex addiction needs you to learn how to form healthy intimacy and connectedness with others. Many addicts make the mistake of thinking that attendance at a 12-step program will give them all the keys to recovery. Remember, the 12-step program is one pillar of this multifaceted wholesome and holistic recovery program.

### *Stop being lazy and do the recovery work*

Stop jumping from one program to another, or blaming programs for your lack of success. Until you reach personal and spiritual awakening, master emotional regulation and take full responsibility for your recovery and your actions, you will stay in the victimhood state where everyone and everything is to be blamed but you.

> **Although 12-step programs are beneficial throughout recovery, they are complementary to therapy, and not the answer to all your personal and relationship difficulties.**

## Compassion Vs Condemnation

Many sex addicts are uncomfortable to sit with their emotions, or in solitude. During active recovery you must learn how not to escape your feelings, and instead face them in a healthy way. This does not happen automatically just because you have stopped your compulsive behaviour. You need to do homework, meditation, exercise, go to therapy on a regular basis, journal and be prepared to put time and energy into your recovery. There isn't a short cut.

### *Remember your limitations and bottom lines*
Know your day to day bottom lines. These are behaviours that subtly fed your addiction. For example, getting lost in movies or scoring those attractive actors, special handshakes, hugging, dressing in a certain way or engaging in chit chat. If you are honest, you will discover your own subtle way of seducing the objects of your attention or feeding your brain with lust. Your behaviours may be unique, so aim to discover them.

### *Cleansing the internal and external environment*
Clean up your thoughts and inner environment as well as people and places around you that may cause you to relapse. People you choose to socialise with must be compatible and respectful of your new clean and healthy lifestyle. And, "no" you are not an exception, you are not superman/superwoman who can still interact with the same toxic/tempting environments or people and manage to stay healthy/sober. The sooner you acknowledge your limitations the faster you will stay true to your effective recovery. You can remove a sick fish from a toxic fish tank, clean it up, care for it until it is healthy. If you put the same fish in a clean tank, it will thrive, but if you put it back into the dirty/toxic tank, it will get sick again. In order for you to thrive, it is your responsibility to clean up your environment.

### Practice humility instead of humiliation

To become humble instead of humiliated requires responsibility. Most addicts are very defensive and feel rejected if they are reminded of any personal flaws. Stay open to welcoming and receiving constructive feedback, recognise your own shortcomings and work on them. Accept that nobody is perfect, including you.

### You are not out of the woods yet

Just because you have been sober from your compulsive sexual behaviours does not make you invincible. You are vulnerable to relapse if you don't take sex addiction seriously or plan ahead for any potential triggers. Many sex addicts feel they have passed the stage of being vigilant and can do the things they stopped doing at the start of their recovery. For example, flirting with others, watching soft pornography, or starting planned masturbations. If only a heroin addict could take a small scheduled amount of heroin, or an alcoholic could still drink a little bit of alcohol, you could be doing the same. However, we know if you or your brain could handle moderation, you would not be here today. Stay humble and recognise your own limitations to stay safe for yourself and others.

### Stop judging others because they are different

You know you still have a long way to recovery if you still silently harbour judgement or resentment towards others. Stop judging other sex addicts, whether male or female. This tendency is due to the mental comparison and judgement you hold. Some sex addicts tend to see themselves as superior and put other sex addicts down, or judge them for their past sexual behaviours. Develop self-esteem, compassion and respect for yourself, and you will be able to project that on to others. Everyone is inherently good and will do their best if favourable conditions are available. What may frighten you is realising that everyone is different. Embrace your – and everyone's – uniqueness. Of all the people who occupy our earth, maybe less than 10% are bad people – the rest are just different people. Seek similarities in others and respect their differences. Don't hold it against them. Human beings have been wrongly conditioned to dislike or be distressed by differences. Others may not share your opinions or values, but that doesn't mean you are wrong or they are wrong. **It simply means we are all different.** There are great learning opportunities in encountering those who are different. Seek to observe similarities while honouring their differences.

Next time you silently judge someone else, stop and ask yourself what is the learning in this for me? I promise there is something valuable you will discover about you.

*Building your self-esteem one day at a time*
For many sex addicts, recovery is about forming the belief that they are essentially good people. This often takes time – but it is achievable – if applying one step at a time and taking one day at a time. Self-esteem is formed when people feel they are doing their best in everything, being true to themselves and following their conscience. Recovering sex addicts need time to process this stage consistently and one day at a time. Building integrity, discipline and persistence in doing the recovery work will add layers to your self-esteem.

*Building your self-esteem can be achieved through the following steps:*
- Decide to recover and make your recovery a priority. Do not ignore the needs of your recovery for the sake of others.

- Commit to your decisions. Once a decision has been made to take a course of action, avoid self-doubt, self-sabotage and second-guessing yourself. Instead put your energy on the necessary steps and work to prioritise your recovery process.

- Stop the "I know best" mentality. Stay open and acknowledge that during recovery, you need others to support you and help you navigate specific issues.

- Stop being a people pleaser. As Sudha Murty once said, "He who tries to please everybody pleases nobody."

- Get to know and honour yourself. As a sex addict, you have most probably spent your whole life disregarding your own needs while acting to be someone else to please others. It is time to discover your authentic self.

- Watch your self-talk. Part of developing healthy self-esteem requires analysing how you talk to yourself and modifying any negative self-talk.

- Foster an attitude of gratitude. Cultivating a healthy sense of self-esteem also involves the ability to be grateful for what you have. This concept seems very easy while it is very effective.

- Develop a positive attitude. Many addicts are stuck in a negative attitude cycle. Changing your self-talk, emphasising your successes over your failures, and being grateful has much to do with maintaining a positive attitude.

- Pick up the courage and learn how to say "No" sometimes. Sex addicts commonly struggle to speak their minds and have learned to be people pleasers. It is time to make your recovery a number one priority and commit to your decisions. Learn to decline requests in an assertive but respectful manner. This will communicate your clear boundaries to others and people will not take advantage of you.

## Compassion Vs Condemnation

Danny Silk (2013, p. 86) author of *Keep your love on: Connection communication and boundaries*, writes:

> *In order for us to practice self-control, we must have a goal. We must have something we are saying "yes" to, which necessarily comes with things that we must say "no" to. We use self-control to manoeuvre ourselves toward this "yes." This goal must be entirely our own. The minute another person is choosing and managing our goals for us, we have left self-control behind.*

- Learn to experience self-love and self-respect in a non-arrogant way. To increase your self-esteem, you need to develop self-love. This does not refer to Narcissus who loves his own reflection; instead self-love emerges from supporting your own values and integrity, and appreciating your own worth. Nurture these traits within yourself.

- Become someone who is generous to others. Although making your needs and recovery priorities, learning to say no, having self-love and forming boundaries are essential, these choices do not require you to disengage and shut others out. Be generous with your time, knowledge and support others when you can.

- Instead of beating yourself up, learn from past mistakes or past relapses. Stop dwelling on the past as some sort of personal punishment. Start viewing these past situations as opportunities to relapse-proof your recovery journey and improve yourself. Changing your thinking will change how you feel, which will change your behaviour. Finally, changing the way you think will raise your self-esteem.

- Acknowledge your successes. Write your successes down and reflect on small wins.

It is crucial to reach a radical acceptance about yourself and your past. Sex addiction may have led you to reckless acts and outrageous behaviour, but now it is important to tell yourself that you are essentially a good human being. Your behaviours and attitudes can be changed, but past is in the past and cannot be undone. Focus on the present moment and change what you can change, instead of wasting time and energy dwelling on the past.

Addiction is a way to numb the emotions, and an excuse to act like someone else. Once the recovery begins, the old person is changing to a new one. Others may not recognise or see the changes right away, but through demonstrating consistent healthy behaviours, others will gradually witness the positive changes. Research has found that self-forgiveness makes people less likely to engage in compulsive sexual behaviours in the future. This buffering effect is because self-forgiveness alleviates current feelings of shame, depression and false guilt.

Practice humility while going through the self-forgiveness stage. Humility will give you an attitude of openness and empathy, and pushes you to keep learning about your shortcomings or attributes while avoiding defensiveness or unfounded pride. The good news is that research has shown that once sex addicts recover, they can turn their lives around. They become productive and respectful members of society. **Recovered sex addicts are great romantic partners, responsible fathers and excellent human beings.**

Self-forgiveness is a prerequisite to effective recovery and can be achieved by engaging in therapy. Seeking the forgiveness of others starts with self-forgiveness. If you cannot forgive yourself, how can others offer you their forgiveness?

CHAPTER 17

# Entering An Intimate Relationship In Recovery

Sex addicts must be stable in recovery before starting a serious relationship.

Establishing friendships at work is different from romantic dating during the early recovery stages. Before attempting to develop a serious relationship, it is crucial that one pauses and assesses the level of recovery. Intimate relationships can impact the individual's feelings and therefore, their sobriety ability. The recovering individual must have developed strength and resilience to withstand the ups and downs that are imminent in every new romance.

Living a clean life makes you ready for your next relationship. However, it would help if you learned to be comfortable being alone, in solitude. Dealing with feelings as they surface and developing new habits all require attention and quality time. A common characteristic of sex addicts is discomfort in being alone and mastering emotional regulation. At the beginning of recovery, often individuals are yearning for relationships and companionship. Once again, this could be, in fact, due to the discomfort of being alone – a scary concept for sex addicts. For others, they believe that if they have a partner, they can recover easier and avoid relapse while receiving legitimate sexual release with a committed partner (object relationship mentality). Many sex addicts find during recovery that once they resist the thrill of compulsive or random sexual activities, they feel disappointed for not experiencing the adrenaline rush every time they meet a potential partner. Sex addiction recovery is about learning to build healthy human relationships, and this is a process that requires intentional efforts and ongoing honest communication with the potential partner and other safe people.

Engaging too soon in sexual intimacy without building any emotional intimacy will lead to more disappointment and more emotional emptiness. Here the sex addict is acting impatiently and according to the old behavioural patterns. To share fears, doubts, insecurities, and vulnerability with a potential partner will provide a healthy relational environment where both partners can work through issues together and become more intimate.

Notably, in the early stages of recovery while the initial adrenaline rushes enhance the enthusiasm towards recovery and its boundless possibilities, it can feel lonely. Feeling loved and cared for are essential human needs and required for overall wellbeing. During recovery individuals may feel the urgency of being loved to form new authentic and passionate relationships. However, as mentioned earlier, entering new intimate relationships during early recovery and before reaching an active recovery stage – before building an authentic relationship with self – can be a gross mistake. The most important relationship that a person must form during recovery is with the body and mind of one's self. Many sex addicts attempt to enter romantic relationships prematurely and find that the stress and anxiety attached to a new relationship cause them to relapse. However, waiting until the sex addict has mastered emotional regulation and has built strong boundaries, both personally and for sobriety, is essential.

Moving through the effective recovery process helps the addicts to develop greater self-awareness, more empathy and compassion for self and others, increased honesty, integrity, and a longing to be responsible and accountable. As these individuals become more aware of their worthiness, they heal their intimacy avoidance and grow the desire to become more vulnerable with others. During recovery sex addicts learn not to escape their emotions. They grow the ability to share their feelings, ambiguity and communicate their needs in a healthy way. In this context, they also learn that relationships are valuable – but not necessary for survival, or to feel good about themselves.

> **Once a recovering addict has reached the point of self-awareness, empathy for self and others, emotional regulation, healthy boundaries, authenticity and self-validation and desires to form a romantic relationship, some factors may need to be considered. A richer and nurturing emotional and sexual intimacy with another person is possible. However, the addict needs to have formed a healthy relationship with self, and having experienced profound solitude. The ex-addict needs to lead a clean life, and to practise ongoing emotional regulation and self-soothing.**

**Checklist for when the recovering addict is ready for a romantic relationship include:**

- When he/she is actively engaged in recovery process and continues with a support group, recovery partner(s) and sponsor.

- When he/she has evolved and developed more awareness of his or her emotions and is able to authentically and willingly talk about them to others.

- When he/she knows how to set healthy boundaries. Setting healthy boundaries in romantic relationships is essential. It is the individual's sole responsibility to set their boundaries and respect boundaries set by others. In healthy relationships, individuals should always be specific and clear about their needs and readily honour the needs of others.

- When he/she learns self-control during recovery process. Solid awareness of self-control is essential during recovery and in establishing new relationships with self and others. Self-control is a way of safeguarding one's mental health. This awareness is vital particularly in situations when the addict may find themselves faced with temptation which can lead to relapse.

- When he/she has learned healthy communication skills. Possessing excellent communication skills are essential when embarking in new healthy relationships. Healthy communication skills require honesty, openness, taking responsibility and being accountable for one's feelings and thoughts.

## Entering An Intimate Relationship In Recovery

- When he/she is comfortable to reach out to others when urges or emotions or challenges in close relationships emerge.

- When he/she has accepted any co-occurring mental diseases that may be existing and is actively working on them during recovery process – attending therapy and doctors on a regular basis. If medications have been given, to ensure their safe use.

- When he /she has been screened and treated for STIs, and is willing to be transparent about STI history, and willing to share this history with any potential future partner before engaging in any sexual activity with them.

- When he/she desires a relationship to add value to life and not out of need or desperation.

- When he/she does not engage in any manipulative behaviours. Sex addicts are commonly very manipulative. During active addiction, individuals manipulate their loved ones to satisfy their addiction. New healthy relationships must be free from any manipulation otherwise it is not a healthy environment for anyone.

- When he/she knows how to avoid deception and dishonesty, and is open, authentic, honest and trustworthy with self and others.

- When he/she has reasonable and honest expectations. One of the common challenges or mistakes in forming new relationships are unreasonable expectations which almost always lead to disappointment. Individuals seeking new relationships must always be open and honest in their communication and prepared that their expectations may not be met.

- When he/she has reached emotional maturity. This is displayed through expressing one's thoughts and feelings with openness, transparency and honesty.

- When he/she avoids making assumptions about self and other's thoughts and feelings as that may trigger a relapse.

- When he/she has developed a relationship with a higher power and is growing spiritually.

- When he/she is willing to be vulnerable and ask for help when it is needed because self-trust and humility have been restored.

- When he/she has left behind obsessions about sex or romance or any emotional co-dependency.

- When he/she has learned how to protect their recovery and avoids emotional, physical and spiritual risky situations.

- When he/she has learned consistent and healthy self-care practices.

- When he/she is comfortable to face negative emotions and go through uncomfortable growing pains for the sake of transformational comfort.

- When he/she is able to stay in solitude with feelings instead of escaping them.

## Entering An Intimate Relationship In Recovery

- When he/she has stopped objectifying or sexualising the potential future partner, and instead of an object relationship, looks for a human relationship.

CHAPTER 18

# Real People, Real Stories

Sex addiction brings a very particular set of challenges and also trauma for both the addict and their partner (family). The discovery of the addictive behaviour is usually a bombshell for the addict's partner. One day life is relatively normal and then the next day they find pornography on the computer, or that the person they are with has been regularly meeting others for sex. It comes as such a shock, and can destroy them psychologically, physically and spiritually. Everyone impacted needs to go through therapy and healing.

Partners (family) usually have lots of questions that there are initially no clear answers to, and they attempt to make sense of something that does not even make sense for the addict themselves. Addicts must seek support and therapy for themselves and help partners/

family in their healing journey too. However, partners must take responsibility for their wellbeing and be careful of their own mental health because it can take a massive toll.

Here are some stories told by sex addicts and their families, in their own words:

## *Ethan (sex addict)*

I am only 26 years old and have the most beautiful fiancée, yet I am unable to be aroused with her. She doesn't have a clue that I have to close my eyes and fantasise about pornographic images in order to orgasm. Many times, I have to think about her friends, my co-workers or even strangers I have seen. Many times she tries to initiate sex, but I am unable to reciprocate because I have not filled my fantasy storage with current images. She deserves more than this, but I have always felt trapped and like a hostage to my own head. All the secrecy, shame and dishonesty was eating me alive until I decided that enough was enough. I sought therapy on my own but I would constantly relapse. Then I thought I would try the 12-step program, and yet I would relapse. One day after talking to my therapist I decided to pick up the courage and tell my fiancée about my porn addiction. I just told her a very diluted version of reality. To say that she was devastated is an understatement. However, she gave me what I exactly needed. She did not take my BS anymore and forced us to seek help together. She researched about it all and soon with the help of our therapist, she could handle all the truth that I had to disclose to her. I still kept some stuff for myself because I was adamant that I would lose her if she found out about the extent of my addiction. But when the therapist and she agreed on a date for my polygraph test, I could not hide any more.

I disclosed everything first to the therapist and she prepared my fiancée, slowly before I gave her the big picture. We had a few rough weeks when I thought for sure I had lost her, but to my amazement every time I dropped my defensiveness and acknowledged her pain instead, things would turn out for the good. The polygraph test was what I needed to be honest with myself and with everyone around me. I had to even confess to my sponsor that I had not told him everything. The freedom I felt was indescribable. At last I was free. It has been two years and we are still in therapy, but life is very sweet these days. We are planning our wedding and we are closer than ever before. These days having sexual intimacy is completely different and doesn't leave me with more cravings or more emptiness. I have learned to be vulnerable and reach out when I need help. I do not live in my head anymore and I live in the present. I remember that I am a recovering addict and acknowledge my limitations every day. This way has brought safety to my partner, and my sobriety. I am not invincible and know that I have to work hard for the rest of my life not to put myself in the zone of temptation. I am excited to be emotionally available to my loved ones. Life is still full of challenges but the difference is I am not escaping it – but I am living it.

## *Katherine (wife of a sex addict)*

When I found out about Jonathan's compulsive sexual behaviours, I was disgusted. I kicked him out and didn't want anything to do with him anymore. I told my two grown up kids who reacted equally, with disgust and rejection towards him. My oldest son became physically violent and punched him a few times. Our family was destroyed and it was all his fault. The coming days, weeks and months passed but I was emotionally stuck. I would experience periods of numbness, rage, sadness or deep depression. Jonathan tried to talk to me but I wouldn't listen. My kids didn't want me to interact with him. My parents hated him. Everyone said he was a pervert and scum. Four months later, he begged me to go to therapy with him and I do not know why, but I agreed. I thought that would be my opportunity to abuse him just the way he had abused us. Our therapist started talking about what sex addiction was and how he had a brain chemical imbalance. We touched on his childhood trauma and I got angry. After all, everyone knew about my abusive, shitty life. How come I didn't become scum or a cheater? I must admit once the therapist talked about brain science and research I couldn't disagree. She asked me to have an open mind and avoid going ahead with the divorce until I had dealt with my trauma.

I am glad that I listened. It took me nine months to decide to give us another chance. One day I would wake up and say, "No way, I am out, I can't handle this," and another day I would say, "Maybe I should give this a chance". I was exhausted with the fight within me. I was so resentful for what he had done to me and to us. Our therapist didn't give up on me and welcomed all my conflicting emotions. After nine months I agreed to try a three month reconciliation but with one condition: to stay true to therapy and give it my all.

Now it has been six months and I am doing much better. Jonathan has moved back in and we have started a brand-new relationship. It took a while for my kids to recover, but therapy helped us all. In the past I would think only women with low self-esteem would stay in a relationship like this; but today I have changed my tone. I say now that running away would have been easy, but staying requires strength. In return, we all are receiving healing. Today I say, "I am very glad that I stayed".

## *Matthew (sex addict)*

I have always been very successful in business. I think my high profile job helped me conceal my addiction and double life. To escape a stressful job and marriage, I began engaging more in my sexual activities and worked longer hours to avoid going home and facing my shame. Then I began hiding money to pay for prostitutes until my wife discovered it. I promised to stop, but I couldn't. Instead, I got better at hiding money and became more extreme with sexual activities. I learned new ways of deceiving her and everyone else. When I was at home, I was playing video games. Now I know my brain was either looking for the high through sexual release or the thrill of the games. My bubble burst when my teenage son was expelled from school for possessing pornographic images. We found out that he had known about my sexual activities for some time, and even though he hated me for that, he had become addicted to them too. I thought we had a good relationship; after all, we would always sit and play video games for hours on end together. I couldn't escape reality anymore, and I admitted to my wife that we needed help. My wife, our son and I went to therapy together. We all had individual and joint therapy session. My wife and I had couple's therapy too. My son went through terrible withdrawals not because of his porn addiction but because of his gaming addiction. We both went cold turkey and removed any temptation from our house. I am very proud of my son because he never complained once about not being able to play games or having his internet or phone filtered. I, on the other hand, had more tantrums and resistance along the way. We both are in recovery and trying to build new relationships with ourselves and others. We have a long journey ahead of us but so far, so good.

Dr. Fai Seyed Aghamiri

## *Locky (sex addict)*

I was used to travelling as a sales rep and staying in motels. Over time the pattern of meeting anonymous sex partners through online dating and hook-up sites escalated and became riskier for me. My constant preoccupation with my need for sexual release loaded with denial one day led me to miss an important meeting for the sake of anonymous sex. Every time afterwards I would promise to stop. I would set a date. I would even hit myself for committing the act. Yet I would find myself hooked in another encounter. I am ashamed that I do not even remember some of the ladies' names. For me, it was about getting my fix so I could function and get on with my life.

Missing that important sales meeting was the last straw for my boss. He found out through the motel that I was not alone. He fired me, and I had to confess to my wife. She kicked me out immediately. I must admit I was relieved to be alone because, in my delusional mind, I thought I could now engage in those activities without guilt or shame. I was wrong. My life went downhill fast. Not only was I not enjoying my sexual activities, but I now felt deeper in shame and lonelier than ever. It took me two years of denial and delusion until I got help.

In the meantime, I hurt my wife even more due to my lack of empathy and carelessness. I could not show any emotions and was running from myself and her, thinking that was for the best. Eventually, I begged her for a second chance. She wanted to see me recovered first. I went through recovery and was hopeful that I could beat the beast this time. And I did. Two years later, once I decided to claim my life back, I did.

I am still working on getting my wife to come back, but every day I stay true to my recovery. I am getting closer to her. After six months of constant begging, she has agreed to join me in therapy which is a big step forward. I am glad that I didn't give up on us. I am glad that I didn't believe my own lies and self-pity. I have stopped watching TV, going to the beach, or flirting with women. I have a healthy lifestyle with lots of meditation and mindfulness and I am still going to weekly therapy and 12-step meetings. My life as I knew it is over, thank God. I am learning to embrace the new norm now.

## *Janet (wife of a sex addict)*

My husband was and is my soulmate and best friend. We were married 25 years, with two kids and three beautiful grandkids, when I found out about his sex addiction. He was taking a shower one evening, and I picked up his phone as it received a text message. He would normally take his phone everywhere with him. I saw a sexually explicit message from someone who was saying she was free and was looking forward to their hook up. In disbelief, I went through all the previous messages and found 100s of similar texts from others. I found naked photos exchanged between him and these women. I could not move – I was frozen. I did not recognise the man I had been with for 25 years. Life became a living hell. In the beginning, he tried to minimise and manipulate himself out of it, but I demanded to have everything out in the open. For months he drip-fed me with new information, and every time I was deeper into my trauma and pain. My nightmare did not have an end in sight. My biggest regret is that I involved my parents and my kids into the saga. They all took my side and wanted to crucify him, which I enjoyed in the beginning. However, in hindsight, it would have been better to allow us go through the process first before bringing others into the mix. This delayed and complicated our recovery and my healing. I was against any therapy and believed "his problem, his recovery". I was wrong. I was so deeply traumatised and hurt that without the help and professional support I received I would not be here today.

It has been four years of hard work, therapy and ongoing learning. What helped me was to educate myself about this disease. Yes, I call it a disease because it is. My husband had kept private the abuse and trauma he had endured as a young boy in the hands of his abusive father and then his neighbour. Carrying all the pain and shame had broken him, and sexual release became his medication to soothe himself. I do not give him an excuse, but it is what it is. I took refuge in food and alcohol for many years because of my own unresolved childhood trauma. Once I started bringing compassion into my shattered heart, things changed. My kids and parents needed to be guided by me to accept him back. This was an even bigger challenge, but I was determined to heal my family. We had so much pain and unresolved conflict that had been swept under the rug, and we got the chance to deal with it. But it took a long, long time.

My husband threw himself into weekly therapy and 12-step meetings. I also had weekly individual therapy, and we also had weekly couple's therapy as well. The biggest benefit was that we both saw the same therapist who could work with us and support us towards our goal. We were all on the same page. My husband has been working hard on his honesty and transparency, and I must admit the man I am with is nothing like the previous man. I am proud of him, and us. I still have days when I am triggered but we both have learned how to handle them and move forward in life. Involving my kids and parents was disastrous and I know my husband would not be here today if I had told more people and had not sought professional help.

## *John (sex addict)*

What began with looking at pornography and masturbating 15 years ago, soon intensified and moved to visiting brothels, searches for other women offline and online and endless sexual encounters. Strangely, I felt very lonely and ashamed because I had to hide my sex to protect my image. I became more isolated, withdrew and even avoided people I loved dearly. I was unable to keep a long-term relationship. No one could compete with my mistress (my addiction). In my head I would always find something wrong with a potential girlfriend and use that as an excuse to finish the relationship. Although I was lonely and desired close relationships, I was unable to stop sabotaging them. I lost a few friendships at this time. One true friend reached out to me and I admitted my problems to him and he was the one who found help and therapy for me. I never forget that day. I was so ashamed but desperate for help. I had a hard time with therapy and facing my demons but gave it my all. Eventually, through therapy and the 12-step program I found a few trusted people I could talk to and trust.

Find safe and trusting people and share your struggles with them, because it is a matter of life or death in this addiction.

## *Robert (sex addict)*

I have always struggled with alcohol to cope with daily stress. Alcohol always had control over me and my emotions. I turned into two different people living in one body. A good one and a bad one. I had lost my first marriage and was now in the middle of a second divorce. I knew deep down it was all my fault. I was the one who would push everyone away and never allowed emotional closeness. I did not seek therapy for my sex addiction but for my depression over losing my marriage. I was a coward or maybe in denial. I resented the therapist when she suggested that I may be the problem, and asked if I had problems with alcohol or any other addictions. I was thinking, "How dare you? I am paying you and I call the shots." She suggested that I join AA meetings. It took me three months to pick up the courage and do that. But I was still not ready to face my sex addiction.

Now trying to stay sober from alcohol pushed me further into porn, masturbation and seeking sex workers. The support and brotherhood I received at AA gave me the courage to open up to my sponsor and tell him about my sex addiction. To my surprise, he said that many AA members do actually suffer from sex addiction, and these two frequently co-exist. The next visit to my therapist, I admitted to my sex addiction. That was the first day of my sobriety. I must say I still resist what my therapist or sponsor say at times and like to design a sobriety program for myself. But I understand this is because I hate discipline and structure, and once again, my brain wants to sabotage it. I must say I did manage to reconcile with my wife. This was not an easy task but eventually was possible. It has been a few blissful years with my wife, and we are both very happy. Although we are still in therapy, our life is manageable, and we have learned how to navigate life's challenges. I am grateful for my sobriety.

## *Niki (female sex addict)*

When I was 12 years old, my teenage cousin, who was 17 years old, sexually molested me. I was so scared and confused that I didn't say anything. Slowly he would get me to watch porn with him and would do the same things that we saw on those images. One day he brought someone else with him and they each had a turn. I was given money or small gifts afterwards. Because he was family my parents never suspected us hanging out so much or going out together. He was seen as a protective older brother. My grades were impacted and at school I would only hang out with bad boys. Soon I learned how to get attention: be promiscuous. I built a reputation of being the weird, horny girl. I hated my life but couldn't stop. At the age of 15, I fell pregnant to one of the customers that my cousin had brought. He helped me to get an abortion and that was the turning point for me, or at least I thought so. After my abortion I couldn't continue school and fell into a deep depression. I was in and out of the hospital while no one knew my story. When I was 17, I moved out of the house with my girlfriend. The thought of being with a man was revolting and I only felt safe with women. Our relationship was volatile and I was suffering. I was masturbating a few times a day and couldn't function without it. Self-satisfaction had become my medication of choice while I wouldn't allow my girlfriend to be intimate too often. Watching porn and participating on chatlines and dating sites became the only way to escape my pain and numb myself. I lost my grip and tried to kill myself. My parents came and took me back home. My mother forced me to go to therapy. This time everything was different. I wanted to share my story. I had hit rock bottom. I am glad to say that this was six months ago and I am in intensive therapy and take some medication to help me with my anxiety. I feel the stigma from society and even other sex addicts. Society looks at sex addicts as monsters but for me I am even rejected among other sex addicts. The majority of addicts are men and there are just a few women. I feel that it is only within the space of my therapy that I can find peace and healing. I wish society would accept that we are human beings and not monsters. And I wish people would accept that I am not a whore but a wounded soul.

## Susan (wife of a sex addict)

I have learned and believe that sex addiction isn't always about love or having sex with someone. it can be secretive regular masturbation happening in the shower or watching pornography in the room right next door. I knew there was something wrong with my husband and our relationship, but I couldn't put my finger on it. We would have long gaps between our sexual intimacy. Therapy wouldn't take us anywhere because he was not truthful about his addiction. How can you fix a problem if you don't acknowledge it? I learned to live in a dysfunctional relationship and lied to myself that he wasn't a terrible man after all. One day I stumbled across his internet history and was shocked at what I found. I tried to confront him. However, he gaslighted me and made me feel bad because "all men were doing that". He said he was watching porn to spice up our sex life and bring back the passion. I felt bad and guilty for making him out to be the bad guy. He promised not to watch porn anymore now that he knew how I felt about it. It was two years later when I found more porn and naked photos of men and women on his computer. I was shattered. How could I compete with both men and women?

I looked at him as a monster. I was disgusted and planned a revenge affair with his best friend. I had my revenge affair which was the biggest mistake of my entire life. I slept with his best friend and felt even cheaper and more humiliated. I felt we both had sunk so low that there was no other option except separation. Our boy couldn't understand why Daddy couldn't see him. My father wanted me to divorce him as soon as possible. My mother took me aside and told me that my own father had had the same problem for years with endless sexual encounters and affairs. She said that my father had not agreed to get help and their marriage had always been superficial and fake. She encouraged me to seek help and give it my best shot before giving up. My husband was willing to do anything but he was struggling with relapse and every time we had an argument or a hiccup, he would relapse and masturbate. Through therapy I found how to set boundaries and how to use a polygraph test to feel safe in my relationship until he was healthy enough to ensure my safety.

We are 12 months into our intensive journey and I must say we are back to living together and have resumed our sexual intimacy. Our connection is completely different and I feel he is present with me. He went through terrible withdrawals and had to go through a polygraph test before I went back to him. I am glad we are still together and very hopeful for our future. I pray that my father would get help soon.

## *Jonathan (sex and love addict)*

My exposure to porn was at an early age. I was seven or eight when I found my father's hidden magazines: Playboy, Penthouse and Hustler. They were hidden under the bed. When my parents were out, the whole ritual of bringing the magazines out, looking at the images and then carefully putting them back became a regular thrill. Every time I knew my parents would leave the house I would go into a trance and become preoccupied with sexual fantasies and thoughts. I couldn't concentrate on anything else except waiting for my fix. Even though I do not remember having orgasms at that young age, I was still feeling the sensations through my whole body.

The first time I ejaculated took me to a different high. I started touching other younger girls or boys and soon I found myself not being able to sleep unless I masturbated. Strangely I was doing well at school without even making an effort to study. I became a very respectable lawyer working in a prestigious practice. However, my double life was soon to be revealed. To feed my sexual addiction, I had to escalate my behaviour to a more exciting and outrageous acts. Watching porn and masturbation would not satisfy as before, and I needed more.

I became addicted to the attention of sex workers such as escorts, strippers and high-end prostitutes. I was convinced they all loved me and I was special. I was always thinking that I was the one in control and was making them do what I wanted them to do. They did all those acts because I was special and not because that was their job. I constantly deceived myself and others. My addiction cost me money and I was giving expensive gifts to a few high-end workers thinking that would make me look powerful and show them that I was different. Once I saw one of the girls that I had bought a car for in a restaurant with another guy and I was upset. I called her later and asked why she was doing that when she was supposed to be only with me and I was supporting her. She came up with a bunch of lies and how she owed him money etc. I paid her even more to repay her debt. Looking back, I can see that I was addicted to love and to the feel of power.

Unfortunately, I sank so deep that I violated the practice's boundary and not only slept with a client but took some money out without authorisation. I lost my law licence one fateful day and now work as an IT guy. Hitting rock bottom forced me to pause and seek help and re-evaluate my life. I was introduced to therapy, the 12-step program, but most importantly I was introduced to God. Currently it has been a few years since that day and I am still working actively on my sobriety and to help others to reach freedom. I am happily married with two beautiful kids. I was honest with my wife from day one we met and I am honest with my kids so they are informed about the pitfalls of porn and sex addiction in life.

## Clara (wife of a sex addict)

Seven years into my marriage, I started to wonder if my husband had lost interest in sex. I started dressing up and playing roles for him, thinking this is what normal couples do. He'd always go to bed later than me telling me that he had to work or had to catch up with some sermons online. He was a devoted Christian and an active member of our church. So, one day I had a terrible fever and felt like dying. I went to the doctor and after some tests I found out that I had contracted an STD. I almost laughed when the doctor asked me to check with my husband who he had been intimate with unless I had been with someone else. I said you don't know my husband. He is shy and an excellent human being. He would always condemn other men for being unfaithful or betraying their partners. I came home in disbelief but my instinct told me to check his computer. I couldn't get access so I went online and paid someone to break in. I was desperate. Time stopped and I felt as if I left my body and became the observer of a dead person. I couldn't believe what I was seeing. Emails, photos, short videos, gay and lesbian explicit acts, transgender acts and more. I was still hopeful that I was dreaming and he would come home and wake me up.

So, when he sat me down and admitted everything, I went deeper into shock and rage. I am embarrassed to say but I became physical. I believe if I hadn't hurt him, that I would have hurt myself. Immediately he called an older and trusted member of our church who came to our rescue. We heard the term sex addiction for the first time from him. My husband was relieved that at least he knew what was wrong with him, but I was furious because I thought that was his excuse for cheating. However, while my life was falling apart, I started my own research and found out about sex addictions and all the facts. I thought I could have dealt with a heroin addict or an alcoholic – anything but this.

When I looked into the research on sex addiction, I started to believe that my husband's behaviour was compulsive and he had a split personality due to past trauma. On top of my STD, I suffered PTSD symptoms, depression, constant migraines and was diagnosed with an autoimmune disease. I could have allowed myself to fall apart even more but one day I woke up and said "enough is enough". I told him that I was ready to give our marriage one last chance before divorcing him. I am glad to say that it was many years ago. We started therapy together and started our healing journey. Considering what I have been through, I am glad that I stayed. Nowadays we both are different people and are both enjoying a completely different and fulfilling relationship.

"Be joyful in hope, patient in affliction, faithful in prayer".
**Romans 12:12**

CHAPTER 19

# Frequently Asked Questions

*How do I know if I am a sex addict?*

A good indication as to whether any behaviour is addictive or not is to pay attention to any negative consequences or harmful implications. If you still continue the sexual behaviours despite negative consequences, then this may be an indication of sex addiction. These consequences can impact your relationships, your work, studies, finances, health or even cause legal problems. You are a sex addict if your fantasies, preoccupations or sexual activities take lots of your time, energy and focus away from other important aspects of your life. If you must keep your sexual behaviours secretive, if you carry shame after acting out, if you keep promising yourself to stop, yet find yourself repeating the same behaviours, then you may be a sex addict. Sex addiction is an out of control sexual behaviour pattern that the person continues repeating while disregarding the negative consequences.

*Why am I addicted to sex?*

Many people ask why they are addicted to sex and how did they become a sex addict. This question comes up when they realize that sex has more control over their lives than it should have. It is important to understand why and how before you try fighting a sex addiction. The first step is finding professional support and exploring the root causes.

*What is the role of pornography in sex addiction?*

Many sex addicts begin their addiction and maintain it through viewing pornography and masturbation. These two behaviours go hand in hand while pornography seems to be the cornerstone. Many sex addicts find it challenging to achieve sobriety from this lethal combination. Online pornography is now mainstream and is available, affordable and easily accessible to everyone with a click of a button. Pornography creates an unrealistic fantasy of what a sexual partner should look and act like. It is impossible for the real partners to compete with these fantasies. Pornography users have impressions of other potential partners and may even feel bored with the same real-life partner. Pornography has created object relationships where other people are sex objects – without any real need for genuine connection or intimacy.

## Frequently Asked Questions

Pornography depicts an illusion of willing sexual partners who are eager to please and give satisfaction, and to be treated as objects. Pornography addiction is a serious addiction and a subtype of sexual addiction with the same negative consequences.

*What can I do if I think my partner has a sexual addiction?*

The first best thing is to communicate your observations with your partner. Do not buy into his/her excuses and take effective action. You both need to enter therapy and educate yourself about this condition. Sex addiction, similar to other addictions, involves denial. Sometimes the person does not even know that they have a problem. The majority of sex addicts say they thought their behaviour was normal, and everyone did it, but no one spoke about it. Your partner needs a motivation to stop getting his/her fix. You must set clear boundaries and find emotional support. Preferably you both must attend the same therapist together and have individual sessions too.

*What is the difference between sex addiction and a high sex drive?*

A person who has a high sex drive will feel satisfied after sex. They can take a "no" from an unwilling partner. It is not about getting a "fix" or a "high". If a partner declines sex, a person with high sex drive does not feel rejected. A sex addict doesn't like sex more – he or she just craves it more. Sex is a way to manage anxiety and distress. Sex addicts will have sex with their partners while having sexual fantasies, preoccupations, or engaging in other secretive sexual behaviours.

*Can I only attend a 12-step program without going to therapy and still recover?*

Unfortunately, research has been very clear in this area. Sex addiction is a multifaceted and complex condition and requires a holistic approach. If individuals do not deal with the root cause of their addiction, or don't learn how to deal with uncomfortable feelings, true and long-lasting recovery will be impossible to achieve. 12-step programs are necessary for recovery, but are not a complete package. Sex addicts need to attend therapy for a few years during recovery to learn how to navigate personal, relational or spiritual challenges. Dr Patrick Carnes, Dr Robert Weiss and Dr Douglas Weiss are all pioneers in sex addiction recovery and they always nominate therapy as the first requirement towards effective and long-lasting recovery. Addicts need to attend therapy and effective 12-step programs during recovery.

*If he loved me, he wouldn't do this to me or our relationship, would he?*

Sex addiction has nothing to do with love. It is about getting high and getting a fix. Like other addictive behaviours such as gambling, drinking, and eating disorders, sex addiction is about coping with emotions. Root causes of sex addiction are multifaceted and complex, and that is the reason why individual and couple's therapy are essential.

*Can a sex addiction be cured?*

Yes, similar to other addictions, sex addiction can be eliminated. However, just like other addictions this requires self-control, maintenance and ongoing healthy life choices. Recovery needs daily motivation and planning to cope with potential triggers or dangerous situations that can jeopardise sobriety. Many sex addicts have recovered and live healthy and productive lives. However, the number one mistake for some is a sense of overconfidence and a premature termination of therapy or other support, which can lead to future problems or relapse.

*Can partners still benefit from therapy, even if the sex addict does not?*

Yes. If the sex addict is in denial or unwilling to receive effective help, it is still vital for the partner to receive help and support. Most partners of sex addicts feel betrayed, angry, abandoned, unloved, manipulated and feel lonely when they are exposed to their partner's sex addiction. These feelings must be dealt with in therapy so healing can start. Partners who ignore their own healing may have a higher risk of increased alcohol consumption, eating disorders, compulsive spending, etc.

*Was it my fault that he is a sex addict?*

Not at all. Research has shown that sex addiction has its roots in childhood or early adolescence. It commonly predates adult relationships. Your partner's sex addiction started before he or she met you. They brought this disease with them into the relationship, you just didn't know about it.

*Can women be sex addicts or is it just men?*

Both men and women can become sex addicts. Sex addiction is not gender-exclusive. Although men vastly outnumber women, recently research has found the numbers of women with sex addiction growing significantly. Increased pornography use has been blamed for this. Female sex addiction involves the same behaviours as male sex addiction. These behaviours include masturbation, pornography consumption, phone sex, anonymous encounters and affairs.

# About The Author

Dr Fai is a skilled and empathic professional counsellor and psychotherapist, supporting adolescents, adults, couples and families. She has more than two decades of clinical experience, both in the UK and Australia, having graduated from the Karolinska Institute of Stockholm, Sweden, as an accomplished dental/oral surgeon.

## Dr. Fai Seyed Aghamiri

Dr Fai has built and owned multiple successful medical practices before deciding to pursue her true passion for counselling and psychotherapy. Currently she practices from two different locations, one in Brisbane and another in Beachmere, Queensland.

She is passionate about relationships and believes that learning to form a healthy and compassionate relationship with ourselves, is the first step in connecting with others. Trust-building and the client's wellbeing are her priorities and a major part of the framework of her practice. She is the principal therapist and director of House of Hope Counselling and Psychotherapy Centre in Brisbane, Australia.

Dr Fai has worked for many years with sex addicts and their partners and is compassionate and passionate to make their voices heard.

She is currently working on her PhD on sex addiction and how it impacts the intimate partner's overall wellness. Concepts such as trauma, low self-esteem and depression experienced by the partners in the aftermath of discovery or disclosure of their partner's sex addiction, are the main topics of her research.

Dr Fai is applying her own design of a framework in dealing with sex addiction and its impact on romantic relationships. She has been very successful in supporting individuals and partners in reconciliation and building new and authentic relationships with the same partners. She is utilising the latest research and neuroscience in her therapy to support healing and recovery. She believes that permanent recovery from sex addiction, both for the individuals and their partners, is absolutely possible. However, she also believes that addiction is a systemic disease, and without the intimate partner's active involvement, true recovery is very difficult, if not impossible.

## About The Author

Her practice experience has shown that her designed framework is very effective, and her step-by-step practical guide for individuals and couples achieves great levels of success. Dr Fai has also designed a strong program for couples facing infidelity or lack of relationship passion that has also been extremely successful. Her next book will be about the intimate partners of sex addicts, and what couples need to do in order to heal and recover from sex addiction.

Dr Fai is zealous about learning and understanding the latest research in her field, and in science, and applies the latest knowledge in her practice. Dr Fai applies multiple methods in dealing with sex addiction. Some of these methods are: talk therapy, art, sand and imagery therapy, EMDR, Neurofeedback, hypnosis, trauma processing, CBT, mindfulness, relationship-building exercises and more. She has a Master's Degree in Counselling and Psychotherapy, as well as many international certifications, and has completed a range of professional training in the field, such as Gottman (level 1, 2), NLP, hypnosis, NeurOptimal® Neurofeedback, EMDR, trauma and PTSD management, infidelity, Gestalt therapy, cognitive behavioural therapy, mindfulness practice, betrayal trauma, ADHD, depression and family therapy.

Dr Fai is a trauma-informed therapist, and therefore, her approach provides safety and empathy necessary for building a strong therapeutic relationship where clients can explore life challenges and reach transformational change. She believes that the mind, body and spirit are interconnected, and therefore, her approach is a holistic one. With her support and unconditional positive regard, clients can safely deal with their past unresolved life challenges or trauma, and experience life's full potential in the present moment.

# Acknowledgements

Many people have encouraged and supported me to gather all my research and information into an easy to understand book. I could not have done this without the support of the sex addicts and their partners. Those are the ones that I like to acknowledge. Their courage, stories and honesty have been inspiring.

I want to recognise Dr. Patrick Carnes and my mentor, Dr Douglas Weiss for what they have done in the field of sex addiction. Through my training as an AASAT therapist, I grew and learned so much more than just what I had read in books. I also like to thank Dr. Johannes Luetz, who has been my educator, my mentor and spiritual support. Dr Luetz has been encouraging me to pursue my academic passion while allowing me space to develop my style.

I would like to acknowledge and thank my beautiful sons Daniel and Robin for being my rocks and not being embarrassed every time I start a conversation about porn or masturbation at gatherings!

Last, but not least, I would like to thank my husband, who has sacrificed many quality times together so I could pursue my dreams. He is my biggest fan and source of encouragement. I could not have done it without you, really.

# Reference list

Adams, K. M. (2008, May 1). Cybersex: The "crack cocaine" of sex addiction. *The National Psychologist.* http://nationalpsychologist.com/2008/05/cybersex-the-'crack-cocaine'-of-sex-addiction/101003.html.

Adams, K. M. (2011). *Silently seduced: When parents make their children partners.* Simon & Schuster.

American Psychiatric Association. (2013). *Diagnostic and Statistical Manual of Mental Disorders (DSM-5®).* American Psychiatric Association Publishing.

American Society of Addiction Medicine. (2011). *The Definition of Addiction.* https://www.asam.org/advocacy/find-a-policy-statement/view-policy-statement/public-policy-statements/2011/12/15/the-definition-of-addiction

Anda, R. F., Felitti, V. J., Bremner, J. D., Walker, J. D., Whitfield, C., Perry, B. D., Dube, S. R., & Giles, W. H. (2005). The enduring effects of abuse and related adverse experiences in childhood. *European Archives of Psychiatry and Clinical Neuroscience, 256*(3), 174-186. https://doi.org/10.1007/s00406-005-0624-4

Angelo, J. (2019, November 4). Are you ready to get real about sex addiction? *National Rehabs Directory.* https://www.rehabs.com/blog/are-you-ready-to-get-real-about-sex-addiction/

Armstrong, A., Quadara, A., El-Murr. A., & Latham, J. (2017). *The effects of pornography on children and young people: An evidence scan.* Australian Institute of Family Studies.

Baltazar, A., Helm, H. W., Mcbride, D., Hopkins, G., & Stevens, J. V. (2010). Internet pornography use in the context of external and internal religiosity. *Journal of Psychology and Theology, 38*(1), 32-40. https://doi:10.1177/009164711003800103

Barna Group. (2017, February 15). How healthy are Pastors' relationships? *Barna.* https://www.barna.com/research/healthy-pastors-relationships/

Berberovic, D. (2013). Sexual compulsivity comorbidity with depression, anxiety, and substance use in students from Serbia and Bosnia and Herzegovina. *Europe's Journal of Psychology, 9*(3), 517-530. https:// doi:10.5964/ejop. v9i3.595.

Berner, W., & Briken, P. (2012). Pleasure seeking and the aspect of longing for an object in perversion. A neuropsychoanalytical perspective. *American Journal of Psychotherapy, 66*(2), 129-150. https://doi.org/10.1176/appi.psychotherapy.2012.66.2.129

Birchard, T. (2004). "The snake and the seraph" – sexual addiction and religious behaviour. *Counselling Psychology Quarterly, 17*(1), 81-88. https://doi:10.1080/0951 5070410001665703

Birchard, T. (2015). *CBT for compulsive sexual behaviour: A guide for professionals.* Routledge.

Blum, K., Chen, A. L., Giordano, J., Borsten, J., Chen, T. J., Hauser, M., Simpatico, T., Femino, J., Braverman, E. R., & Barh, D. (2012). The addictive brain: All roads lead to dopamine. *Journal of Psychoactive Drugs, 44*(2), 134-143. https://doi.org/10.1080/02791072.2012.685407

Brand, M., Young, K. S., & Laier, C. (2014). Prefrontal control and internet addiction: A theoretical model and review of neuropsychological and neuroimaging findings. *Frontiers in Human Neuroscience, 8.* https://doi:10.3389/fnhum.2014.00375

Bronner, G., & Ben-Zion, I. Z. (2014). Unusual masturbatory practice as an etiological factor in the diagnosis and treatment of sexual dysfunction in young men. *The Journal of Sexual Medicine, 11*(7), 1798-1806. https://doi.org/10.1111/jsm.12501

Cameron, C. M., & Carelli, R. M. (2012). Cocaine abstinence alters nucleus accumbens firing dynamics during goal-directed behaviours for cocaine and sucrose. *European Journal of Neuroscience, 35*(6), 940-951. https:// doi:10.1111/j.1460-9568.2012. 08024.x

Carnes P. J. (1991). *Don't call it love: Recovery from sexual addiction.* Bantam Books.

Carnes, P. J. (2009). *Out of the shadows: Understanding sexual addiction.* Simon & Schuster.

Carnes, P. (2012). *A gentle path through the twelve steps: The classic guide for all people in the process of recovery.* Hazelden Publishing.

Carnes, P. J. (2013). *Don't call it love: Recovery from sexual addiction.* Bantam Books.

Carnes, P. J. (2015). The whole and the sum of the parts… Towards a more inclusive understanding of divergences in sexual behaviours. *Sexual Addiction & Compulsivity, 22*(2), 105-108. https://doi:10.1080/10720162.2015.1050329

Carnes, P. J., & Adams, K. M. (2013). *Clinical management of sex addiction.* Routledge.

Carnes, P. J., Delmonico, D. L., & Griffin, E. (2009). *In the shadows of the net: Breaking free of compulsive online sexual behaviour.* Simon & Schuster.

# Reference list

Carnes, P. J., Green, B. A., Merlo, L. J., Polles, A., Carnes, S., & Gold, M. S. (2012). Pathos: A brief screening application for assessing sexual addiction. *Journal of Addiction Medicine*, *6*(1), 29-34. https://doi.org/10.1097/adm.0b013e3182251a28

Carnes, S., & Love, T. (2017). Separating models obscures the scientific underpinnings of sex addiction as a disorder. *Archives of Sexual Behaviour*, *46*(8), 2253-2256. https://doi:10.1007/s10508-017-1072-8

Chamberlain, S. R., Lochner, C., Stein, D. J., Goudriaan, A. E., Van Holst, R. J., Zohar, J., & Grant, J. E. (2016). Behavioural addiction – A rising tide? *European Neuropsychopharmacology*, *26*(5), 841-855. https://doi: 10.1016/j.euroneuro.2015.08.013

Chen, B. T., Bowers, M. S., Martin, M., Hopf, F. W., Guillory, A. M., Carelli, R. M., Bonci, A. (2008). Cocaine but not natural reward self-administration nor passive cocaine infusion produces persistent LTP in the VTA. *Neuron*, *59*(2), 288-297. https://doi: 10.1016/j.neuron.2008.05.024

Coleman, E. (1992). Is your patient suffering from compulsive sexual behaviour? *Psychiatric Annals*, *22*(6), 320-325. https://doi:10.3928/0048-5713-19920601-09

Coleman, E. (2012). Impulsive/compulsive sexual behaviour: Assessment and treatment. *Oxford Handbooks Online*. https:// doi:10.1093/oxfordhb/9780195389715.013.0108

Collins, P., & Collins, G. N. (2011). *A couple's guide to sexual addiction: A step-by-step plan to rebuild trust and restore intimacy.* Simon & Schuster.

Cooper, A. (1997). The internet and sexuality: Into the next millenium. *Journal of Sex Education and Therapy*, *22*(1), 5-6. https://doi:10.1080/01614576.1997.11074164

Corne, S., Briere, J., & Esses, L. M. (1992). Women's attitudes and fantasies about rape as a function of early exposure to pornography. *Journal of Interpersonal Violence*, *7*(4), 454-461. https://doi.org/10.1177/088626092007004002

Cox, R. P., & Howard, M. D. (2007). Utilization of EMDR in the treatment of sexual addiction: A case study. *Sexual Addiction & Compulsivity*, *14*(1), 1-20. https://doi: 10.1080/10720160601011299

Cusimano, A. (2018). EMDR in the treatment of adolescent obsessive-compulsive disorder: A case study. *Journal of EMDR Practice and Research*, *12*(4), 242-254. https://doi.org/10.1891/1933-3196.12.4.242

De Alarcón, R., De la Iglesia, J., Casado, N., & Montejo, A. (2019). Online porn addiction: What we know and what we don't – a systematic review. *Journal of Clinical Medicine*, *8*(1), 91. https://doi:10.3390/jcm8010091

Delmonico, D. L., & Griffin, E. J. (2011). Cybersex addiction and compulsivity. In K.S. Young & C. N de Abreu (Eds.), *Internet Addiction, A handbook and guide to evaluation and treatment.* (pp.113-134). Wiley. https://doi.org/10.1002/9781118013991.ch7

Delmonico, D., & Miller, J. (2003). The internet sex screening test: A comparison of sexual compulsives versus non-sexual compulsives. *Sexual and Relationship Therapy*, *18*(3), 261-276. https://doi.org/10.1080/1468199031000153900

Dodge, B., Reece, M., Cole, S. L., & Sandfort, T. G. (2004). Sexual compulsivity among heterosexual college students. *Journal of Sex Research*, *41*(4), 343-350. https://doi:10.1080/00224490409552241

Doidge, N. (2008). *The brain that changes itself: Stories of personal triumph from the frontiers of brain science*. Penguin.

Donaldson, A. A., Lindberg, L. D., Ellen, J. M., & Marcell, A. V. (2013). Receipt of sexual health information from parents, teachers, and healthcare providers by sexually experienced U.S. adolescents. *Journal of Adolescent Health*, *53*(2), 235-240. https://doi: 10.1016/j.jadohealth.2013.03.017

Dube, S. R., Felitti, V. J., Dong, M., Chapman, D. P., Giles, W. H., & Anda, R. F. (2003). Childhood abuse, neglect, and household dysfunction and the risk of illicit drug use: The adverse childhood experiences study. *Pediatrics*, *111*(3), 564-572. https://doi.org/10.1542/peds.111.3.564

El-Murr, A. (2017). *Problem sexual behaviours and sexually abusive behaviours in Australian children and young people*. Australian Institute of Family Studies. https://aifs.gov.au/cfca/publications/problem-sexual-behaviours-and-sexually-abusive-behaviours-australian-children

Erez, G., Pilver, C., & Potenza, M. (2016). Gender-related differences in the associations between sexual impulsivity, psychiatric disorders and trauma. *European Psychiatry*, *33*, S42. https://doi: 10.1016/j.eurpsy.2016.01.893

Estellon, V., & Mouras, H. (2012). Sexual addiction: Insights from psychoanalysis and functional neuroimaging. *Socioaffective Neuroscience & Psychology*, 2(1), 11814. https://doi.org/10.3402/snp.v2i0.11814

Ey, L-a., McInnes, E., & Rigney, L. I. (2017). Educators' understanding of young children's typical and problematic sexual behaviour and their training in this area. *Sex Education*, 17(6), 682-696. https://doi:10.1080/14681811.2017.1357030

Ey, L., & McInnes, E. (2017). Educators' observations of children's display of problematic sexual behaviors in educational settings. *Journal of Child Sexual Abuse*, 27(1), 88-105. https://doi:10.1080/10538712.2017.1349855

Fairley, M. (2018). *The M Word: Christianity, Masturbation and Porn*. Independently published.

Fileborn, B. (2016). Justice 2.0: Street harassment victims' use of social media and online activism as sites of informal justice. *British Journal of Criminology*, 57(6), 1482-1501. https://doi.org/10.1093/bjc/azw093

Foubert, J. (2019, September 17). *Truth About Porn*. [Video] YouTube. https://www.youtube.com/watch?v=oPxnmgOO06w

Frankl, V. (1959). *Man's search for meaning*. 2nd ed. Beacon Press.

Fries, D. (2018, October 8). 12 simple activities you can do to start building self-esteem today. *Psych Central*. https://psychcentral.com/lib/12-simple-activities-you-can-do-to-start-building-self-esteem-today/

# Reference list

Frohmader, K., Wiskerke, J., Wise, R., Lehman, M., & Coolen, L. (2010). Methamphetamine acts on subpopulations of neurons regulating sexual behaviour in male rats. *Neuroscience, 166*(3), 771-784.https:// doi: 10.1016/j.neuroscience.2009.12.070

Garcia, F. D., & Thibaut, F. (2010). Sexual addictions. *The American Journal of Drug and Alcohol Abuse, 36*(5), 254-260. https://doi:10.3109/00952990.2010.503823

Georgiadis, J., & Kringelbach, M. (2012). The human sexual response cycle: Brain imaging evidence linking sex to other pleasures. *Progress in Neurobiology, 98*(1), 49-81. https://doi.org/10.1016/j.pneurobio.2012.05.004

Gola, M., Lewczuk, K., & Skorko, M. (2016). What matters: Quantity or quality of pornography use? Psychological and behavioral factors of seeking treatment for problematic pornography use. *The Journal of Sexual Medicine, 13*(5), 815-824. https:// doi: 10.1016/j.jsxm.2016.02.169

Goodman, A. (1993). Diagnosis and treatment of sexual addiction. *Journal of Sex & Marital Therapy, 19*(3), 225-251. https://doi:10.1080/00926239308404908

Griffiths, M. D. (2011). Internet sex addiction: A review of empirical research. *Addiction Research & Theory, 20*(2), 111-124. https://doi:10.3109/16066359.2011.588351

Grubbs, J. B., Exline, J. J., Pargament, K. I., Hook, J. N., & Carlisle, R. D. (2015). Transgression as addiction: Religiosity and moral disapproval as predictors of perceived addiction to pornography. *Archives of Sexual Behavior, 44*(1), 125-136. https://doi:10.1007/s10508-013-0257-z

Grubbs, J. B., Volk, F., Exline, J. J., & Pargament, K. I. (2013). Internet pornography use: Perceived addiction, psychological distress, and the validation of a brief measure. *Journal of Sex & Marital Therapy, 41*(1), 83-106.

https://doi.org/10.1080/0092623x.2013.842192

Gwinn, A. M., Lambert, N. M., Fincham, F. D., & Maner, J. K. (2013). Pornography, relationship alternatives, and intimate extradyadic behavior. *Social Psychological and Personality Science, 4*(6), 699-704. https://doi.org/10.1177/1948550613480821

Haber, D. (2010, April 10). Sex addiction: Yearning for the connection you fear most. *Good Therapy*. https://www.goodtherapy.org/blog/sex-addiction-double-bind/

Hall, P. (2011). A biopsychosocial view of sex addiction. *Sexual and Relationship Therapy, 26*(3), 217-228. https://doi:10.1080/14681994.2011.628310

Hall, P. (2018). Female sex and love addiction. In *Understanding and Treating Sex and Pornography Addiction*, (pp. 73-78). Routledge

Hatch, L. (2019, December 17). Mindfulness and brain changes in sex addiction relapse prevention. *PsychCentral*. https://blogs.psychcentral.com/sex-addiction/2014/03/meditation-mindfulness-and-prayer-in-sex-addiction-relapse-prevention/

Hilton, D. L. (2013). Pornography addiction – a supranormal stimulus considered in the context of neuroplasticity. *Socioaffective Neuroscience & Psychology, 3*(1), 20767. https://doi.org/10.3402/snp.v3i0.20767

Hook, J. N., Farrell, J. E., Davis, D. E., Van Tongeren, D. R., Griffin, B. J., Grubbs, J., Penberthy, J. K., & Bedics, J. D. (2015). Self-forgiveness and hypersexual behaviour. *Sexual Addiction & Compulsivity, 22*(1), 59-70. https://doi.org/10.1080/10720162.2014.1001542

Hyman, S. E. (2005). Addiction: A disease of learning and memory. *American Journal of Psychiatry, 162*(8), 1414-1422. https://doi: 10.1176/appi.ajp.162.8.1414

Ioannidis, K., Treder, M. S., Chamberlain, S. R., Kiraly, F., Redden, S. A., Stein, D. J. & Grant, J. E. (2018). Problematic internet use as an age-related multifaceted problem: Evidence from a two-site survey. *Addictive Behaviours, 81*, 157-166.

https:// doi: 10.1016/j.addbeh.2018.02.017

Irvine, J. M. (1993). Regulated passions: The invention of inhibited sexual desire and sex addiction. *Social Text*, (37), 203. https:// doi:10.2307/466269

Johns, J. (2020). False self. https://www.encyclopedia.com/psychology/dictionaries-thesauruses-pictures-and-press-releases/false-self

Kafka, M. P. (2010). Hypersexual disorder: A proposed diagnosis for DSM-V. *Archives of Sexual Behaviour, 39*(2), 377-400. https://doi.org/10.1007/s10508-009-9574-7

Kafka, M. P., & Krueger, R. B. (2011). Response to Moser's (2010) critique of hypersexual disorder for DSM-5. *Archives of Sexual Behaviour, 40*(2), 231-232. https://doi:10.1007/s10508-011-9740-6

Kaplan, M. S., & Krueger, R. B. (2010). Diagnosis, assessment and treatment of hypersexuality. *Journal of Sex Research, 47*(2-3), 181-198. https://doi:10.1080/00224491003592863

Kaplan, D. (2014, January 5). EMDR and Sex Addiction. Debra L. Kaplan. https://debrakaplancounseling.com/emdr-and-sex-addiction/

Karila, L., Wery, A., Weinstein, A., Cottencin, O., Petit, A., Reynaud, M., & Billieux, J. (2014). Sexual addiction or hypersexual disorder: different terms for the same problem? a review of the literature. *Current Pharmaceutical Design, 20*(25), 4012-4020. https://doi:10.2174/13816128113199990619

Katehakis, A. (2019, November 15). It looks like 'Gaslighting,' but it's NOT: Introducing reflection aggression. *Family Solutions Counselling*. https://familysolutionsok.com/it-looks-like-gaslighting-but-its-not-introducing-reflection-aggression/

Kauer, J. A., & Malenka, R. C. (2007). Synaptic plasticity and addiction. *Nature Reviews Neuroscience, 8*(11), 844-858. https://doi:10.1038/nrn2234

Kaufman, G. (1989). *The psychology of shame*. Routledge.

Kimmel, M. S. (2008). *Guyland: The perilous world where boys become men*. HarperCollins.

Kingston, D. A., & Firestone, P. (2008). Problematic hypersexuality: a review of conceptualization and diagnosis. *Sexual Addiction & Compulsivity, 15*(4), 284-310. https://doi:10.1080/10720160802289249

## Reference list

Kor, A., Fogel, Y., Reid, R. & Potenza, M. (2013). Should hypersexual disorder be classified as an addiction? *Sex Addict Compulsivity, 20*(1-2). https://doi: 10.1080/10720162.2013.768132.

Kraus, S. W., Potenza, M. N., Martino, S., & Grant, J. E. (2015). Examining the psychometric properties of the Yale-Brown Obsessive–Compulsive Scale in a sample of compulsive pornography users. *Comprehensive Psychiatry, 59*, 117-122. https://doi: 10.1016/j.comppsych.2015.02.007

Kraus, S. W., Voon, V., Kor, A., & Potenza, M. N. (2016). Searching for clarity in muddy water: future considerations for classifying compulsive sexual behaviour as an addiction. *Addiction, 111*(12), 2113-2114. https://doi:10.1111/add.13499

Laier, C., Schulte, F. P., & Brand, M. (2013). Pornographic picture processing interferes with working memory performance. *Journal of Sex Research, 50*(7), 642-652. https://doi.org/10.1080/00224499.2012.716873

Lambert, N. M., Negash, S., Stillman, T. F., Olmstead, S. B., & Fincham, F. D. (2012). A love that doesn't last: Pornography consumption and weakened commitment to one's romantic partner. *Journal of Social and Clinical Psychology, 31*(4), 410-438. https://doi.org/10.1521/jscp.2012.31.4.410

Landripet, I., & Štulhofer, A. (2015). Is pornography use associated with sexual difficulties and dysfunctions among younger heterosexual men? *The Journal of Sexual Medicine, 12*(5), 1136-1139. https://doi:10.1111/jsm.12853

Lewis, M. (2012). *Memoirs of an addicted brain: a neuroscientist examines his former life on drugs*. Scribe Publications.

Lobo, D. S., & Kennedy, J. L. (2006). The genetics of gambling and behavioral addictions. *CNS Spectrums, 11*(12), 931-939.

https://doi.org/10.1017/s1092852900015121

Love, T., Laier, C., Brand, M., Hatch, L., & Hajela, R. (2015). Neuroscience of internet pornography addiction: A review and update. *Behavioral Sciences, 5*(3), 388-433. https://doi.org/10.3390/bs5030388

Maas, M. K., Vasilenko, S. A., & Willoughby, B. J. (2018). A dyadic approach to pornography use and relationship satisfaction among heterosexual couples: the role of pornography acceptance and anxious attachment. *The Journal of Sex Research, 55*(6), 772-782. https://doi:10.1080/00224499.2018.1440281

Maddox, A. M., Rhoades, G. K., & Markman, H. J. (2009). Viewing sexually-explicit materials alone or together: Associations with relationship quality. *Archives of Sexual Behavior, 40*(2), 441-448. https://doi.org/10.1007/s10508-009-9585-4

Martin, R. A., MacKinnon, S., Johnson, J., & Rohsenow, D. J. (2011). Purpose in life predicts treatment outcome among adult cocaine abusers in treatment. *Journal of Substance Abuse Treatment, 40*(2), 183-188. https://doi.org/10.1016/j.jsat.2010.10.002

Martino, S. C., Elliott, M. N., Corona, R., Kanouse, D. E., & Schuster, M. A. (2008). Beyond the 'Big Talk': The roles of breadth and repetition in parent-adolescent communication about sexual topics. *Pediatrics, 121*(3), e612-e618. https://doi:10.1542/peds.2007-2156

Mate, G. (2019). Human development through the lens of science and compassion. *Dr. Gabor Mate.* https://drgabormate.com/

Menassa, B. M., Holden, J. M., & Bevly, C. M. (2015). Sex addiction and propensity for boundary violation: exploring correlation and change over time. *Sexual Addiction & Compulsivity, 22*(4), 290-313. https://doi:10.1080/10720162.2015.1072488

Miller, R. (2012). Treatment of behavioral addictions utilizing the feeling-state addiction protocol: A multiple baseline study. *Journal of EMDR Practice and Research, 6*(4), 159-169. https://doi.org/10.1891/1933-3196.6.4.159

Miller, R. (2011). The feeling-state theory of behavioural and substance addictions and the feeling-state addiction protocol. https://emdria.omeka.net/items/show/21439

Miner, M. H., Raymond, N., Mueller, B. A., Lloyd, M., & Lim, K. O. (2009). Preliminary investigation of the impulsive and neuroanatomical characteristics of compulsive sexual behavior. *Psychiatry Research: Neuroimaging, 174*(2), 146-151. https://doi.org/10.1016/j.pscychresns.2009.04.008

Montgomery-Graham, S. (2017). Conceptualization and assessment of hypersexual disorder: a systematic review of the literature. *Sexual Medicine Reviews, 5*(2), 146-162. https://doi: 10.1016/j.sxmr.2016.11.001

Najavits, L., Lung, J., Froias, A., Paull, N., & Bailey, G. (2014). A study of multiple behavioral addictions in a substance abuse sample. *Substance Use & Misuse, 49*(4), 479-484. https://doi:10.3109/10826084.2013.858168

NeurOptimal. (2020). *NeurOptimal®* promotes a flexible-and-resilient mindset, empowering your personal transformation. Neuroptimal. https://neuroptimal.com/

Nouwen, H. (1999). *The inner voice of love.* Image Publishing.

O'Brien, W. (2010). *Australia's response to sexualised or sexually abusive behaviours in children and young people.* Australian Crime Commission. http://hdl.handle.net/10536/DRO/DU:30065114

O'Sullivan, L. F., Brotto, L. A., Byers, E. S., Majerovich, J. A., & Wuest, J. A. (2014). Prevalence and characteristics of sexual functioning among sexually experienced middle to late adolescents. *The Journal of Sexual Medicine, 11*(3), 630-641. https:// doi:10.1111/jsm.12419

Olmstead, S. B., Negash, S., Pasley, K., & Fincham, F. D. (2012). Emerging adults' expectations for pornography use in the context of future committed romantic relationships: A qualitative study. *Archives of Sexual Behavior, 42*(4), 625-635. https://doi.org/10.1007/s10508-012-9986-7

Orford, J. (1978). Hypersexuality: Implications for a theory of dependence. *Addiction, 73*(3), 299-310. https://doi:10.1111/j.1360-0443.1978.tb00157.x

## Reference list

Orzack, M. H., Voluse, A. C., Wolf, D., & Hennen, J. (2006). An ongoing study of group treatment for men involved in problematic internet-enabled sexual behavior. *CyberPsychology & Behaviour, 9*(3), 348-360. https://doi:10.1089/cpb.2006.9.348

Park, B., Wilson, G., Berger, J., Christman, M., Reina, B., Bishop, F., ... Doan, A. (2016). Is internet pornography causing sexual dysfunctions? A review with clinical reports. *Behavioural Sciences, 6*(3), 17. https://doi:10.3390/bs6030017

Park, S. Q., Kahnt, T., Dogan, A., Strang, S., Fehr, E., & Tobler, P. N. (2017). A neural link between generosity and happiness. *Nature Communications, 8*(1). https://doi.org/10.1038/ncomms15964

Perry, J. C., Presniak, M. D., & Olson, T. R. (2013). Defence mechanisms in Schizotypal, borderline, antisocial, and narcissistic personality disorders. *Psychiatry: Interpersonal and Biological Processes, 76*(1), 32-52. https://doi.org/10.1521/psyc.2013.76.1.32

Perry, S. L. (2019). *Addicted to lust: Pornography in the lives of conservative Protestants.* Oxford University Press.

Perry, S. L., & Davis, J. T. (2017). Are pornography users more likely to experience a romantic breakup? Evidence from longitudinal data. *Sexuality & Culture, 21*(4), 1157-1176. https://doi.org/10.1007/s12119-017-9444-8

Perry, S. L., & Hayward, G. M. (2017). Seeing is (not) believing: How viewing pornography shapes the religious lives of young Americans. *Social Forces.* https://doi:10.1093/sf/sow106

Phillips-Farfán, B. V., & Fernández-Guasti, A. (2009). Endocrine, neural and pharmacological aspects of sexual satiety in male rats. *Neuroscience & Biobehavioural Reviews, 33*(3), 442-455. https://doi: 10.1016/j.neubiorev.2008.11.003

Pitchers, K. K., Coppens, C. M., Beloate, L. N., Fuller, J., Van, S., Frohmader, K. S., ... Coolen, L. M. (2014). Endogenous opioid-induced neuroplasticity of dopaminergic neurons in the ventral tegmental area influences natural and opiate reward. *Journal of Neuroscience, 34*(26), 8825-8836.https://doi:10.1523/jneurosci.0133-14.2014

Pitchers, K. K., Vialou, V., Nestler, E. J., Laviolette, S. R., Lehman, M. N., & Coolen, L. M. (2013). Natural and drug rewards act on common neural plasticity mechanisms with FosB as a key mediator. *Journal of Neuroscience, 33*(8), 3434-3442. https://doi:10.1523/jneurosci.4881-12.2013

Pizzol, D., Bertoldo, A., & Foresta, C. (2016). Adolescents and web porn: a new era of sexuality. *International Journal of Adolescent Medicine and Health, 28*(2), 169-73. https://doi:10.1515/ijamh-2015-0003

Pornhub insights. (2018, December 11). 2018 year in review. *Pornhub Insights.* https://www.Pornhub.com/insights/2018-year-in-review

Potenza, M. N. (2014). Non-substance addictive behaviours in the context of DSM-5. *Addictive Behaviours, 39*(1), 1-2. https://doi: 10.1016/j.addbeh.2013.09.004

Price, J., Patterson, R., Regnerus, M., & Walley, J. (2016). How much more XXX is Generation X consuming? Evidence of changing attitudes and behaviours related to pornography since 1973. *The Journal of Sex Research*, *53*(1), 12-20. https://doi:10.1080/00224499.2014.1003773

Quadara, A., Nagy, V., Higgins, D., & Siegel, N. (2015). *Conceptualising the prevention of child sexual abuse: Final report* (Research Report No. 33). Australian Institute of Family Studies.

Regnerus, M., Gordon, D., & Price, J. (2015). Documenting pornography use in America: a comparative analysis of methodological approaches. *The Journal of Sex Research*, *53*(7), 873-881. https://doi:10.1080/00224499.2015.1096886

Reid, R. C. (2015). Additional challenges and issues in classifying compulsive sexual behaviour as an addiction. *Addiction*, *111*(12), 2111-2113. https://doi:10.1111/add.13370

Reid, R. C., Carpenter, B. N., Hook, J. N., Garos, S., Manning, J. C., Gilliland, R., … Fong, T. (2012). Report of findings in a DSM-5 field trial for hypersexual disorder. *The Journal of Sexual Medicine*, *9*(11), 2868-2877. https://doi:10.1111/j.1743-6109.2012.02936.x

Reid, R. C., Karim, R., McCrory, E., & Carpenter, B. N. (2010). Self-reported differences on measures of executive function and hypersexual behaviour in a patient and community sample of men. *International Journal of Neuroscience*, *120*(2), 120-127. https://doi:10.3109/00207450903165577

Rew, L., & Wong, Y. J. (2006). A systematic review of associations among religiosity/spirituality and adolescent health attitudes and behaviours. *Journal of Adolescent Health*, *38*(4), 433-442. https://doi: 10.1016/j.jadohealth.2005.02.004

Riemersma, J., & Sytsma, M. (2013). A new generation of sexual addiction. *Sexual Addiction & Compulsivity*, *20*(4), 306-322. https://doi:10.1080/10720162.2013.843067

Rissel, C., Richters, J., De Visser, R. O., McKee, A., Yeung, A., & Caruana, T. (2016). A profile of pornography users in Australia: findings from the second Australian study of health and relationships. *The Journal of Sex Research*, *54*(2), 227-240. https://doi:10.1080/00224499.2016.1191597

Rosenberg, K. P., O'Connor, S., & Carnes, P. (2014). Sex addiction. *Behavioural Addictions*, 215-236. https://doi:10.1016/b978-0-12-407724-9.00009-4

Salamone, J., & Correa, M. (2012). The mysterious motivational functions of mesolimbic dopamine. *Neuron*, *76*(3), 470-485. https://doi: 10.1016/j.neuron.2012.10.021

Sani, M. N. (2010). Drug addiction among undergraduate students of private universities in Bangladesh. *Procedia - Social and Behavioural Sciences*, *5*, 498-501. https://doi: 10.1016/j.sbspro.2010.07.131

Schiebener, J., Laier, C., & Brand, M. (2015). Getting stuck with pornography? Overuse or neglect of cybersex cues in a multitasking situation is related to symptoms of cybersex addiction. *Journal of Behavioral Addictions*, *4*(1), 14-21. https://doi:10.1556/jba.4.2015.1.5

# Reference list

Schneider, J. P., & Irons, R. (1996). Differential diagnosis of addictive sexual disorders using the dsm-iv. *Sexual Addiction & Compulsivity, 3*(1), 7-21. https://doi:10.1080/10720169608400096

Schnitzius, R. (2019, January 7). The 7 Pillars of Sex Addiction Treatment. *Sex Addict Help.* https://sexaddicthelp.com/author/robert-s/

Schreiber, L. R., Odlaug, B. L., & Grant, J. E. (2012). Compulsive Sexual Behaviour: Phenomenology and Epidemiology. *Oxford Handbooks Online.* https://doi:10.1093/oxfordhb/9780195389715.013.0063

Seok, J., & Sohn, J. (2015). Neural substrates of sexual desire in individuals with problematic hypersexual behaviour. *Frontiers in Behavioural Neuroscience, 9.* https://doi:10.3389/fnbeh.2015.00321

Sherman, J. (2015). *Storytelling: An encyclopedia of mythology and folklore.* Routledge.

Short, M. B., Kasper, T. E., & Wetterneck, C. T. (2015). The relationship between religiosity and internet pornography use. *Journal of Religion and Health, 54*(2), 571-583. https://doi:10.1007/s10943-014-9849-8

Short, M. B., Wetterneck, C. T., Bistricky, S. L., Shutter, T., & Chase, T. E. (2016). Clinicians' beliefs, observations, and treatment effectiveness regarding clients' sexual addiction and internet pornography use. *Community Mental Health Journal, 52*(8), 1070-1081. https://doi:10.1007/s10597-016-0034-2

Siegel, D. J. (2015). *The developing mind: How relationships and the brain interact to shape who we are* (2nd ed.). Guilford Publications.

Silk, D. (2013). *Keep your love on: Connection, communication and boundaries.* Red Arrow Publishing.

Smith, D. E. (2012). Editor's note: The process addictions and the new ASAM definition of addiction. *Journal of Psychoactive Drugs, 44*(1), 1-4. https://doi.org/10.1080/02791072.2012.662105

Smith, P., Potenza, M., Mazure, C., McKee, S., Park, C., & Hoff, R. (2014). Compulsive sexual behaviour among male military veterans: Prevalence and associated clinical factors. *Journal of Behavioral Addictions, 3*(4), 214-222. https://doi:10.1556/jba.3.2014.4.2

Smith, T. (2019). Recovery & Treatment of Sexual Addiction: An Interview with Dr. Patrick Carnes. https://irispublishers.com/oajap/pdf/OAJAP.MS.ID.000549.pdf

Sniewski, L., Farvid, P., & Carter, P. (2018). The assessment and treatment of adult heterosexual men with self-perceived problematic pornography use: A review. *Addictive Behaviors, 77,* 217-224. https://doi: 10.1016/j.addbeh.2017.10.010

Spenhoff, M., Kruger, T. H., Hartmann, U., & Kobs, J. (2013). Hypersexual behaviour in an online sample of males: Associations with personal distress and functional impairment. *The Journal of Sexual Medicine, 10*(12), 2996-3005. https://doi:10.1111/jsm.12160

Sun, C., Bridges, A., Johnson, J. A., & Ezzell, M. B. (2014). Pornography and the male sexual script: An analysis of consumption and sexual relations. *Archives of Sexual Behavior, 45*(4), 983-994. https://doi.org/10.1007/s10508-014-0391-2

Sutton, K. S., Stratton, N., Pytyck, J., Kolla, N. J., & Cantor, J. M. (2015). Patient characteristics by type of hypersexuality referral: A quantitative chart review of 115 consecutive male cases. *Journal of Sex & Marital Therapy, 41*(6), 563-580. https://doi.org/10.1080/0092623x.2014.935539

The Dawn. (2020). The importance of forgiving yourself in addiction recovery. https://thedawnrehab.com/addiction/forgiving-yourself-addiction-treatment/

The Sydney Morning Herald. (2016, March 16). Kids' smartphone usage rampant, says study. https://www.smh.com.au/technology/kids-smartphone-usage-rampant-says-study-20150316-1m0nti.html

Tinbergen, N. (1951). *The study of instinct*. Clarendon Press.

Vancouver Wellness Studio. (2019, June 5). Helping men heal from sex addiction with EMDR trauma treatment. https://vancouverwellnessstudio.com/blog/2019/6/helping-men-heal-from-sex-addiction-with-emdr-trauma-treatment

Vidya, T. N. (2018). Supernormal stimuli and responses. *Resonance, 23*(8), 853-860. https://doi.org/10.1007/s12045-018-0688-x

Villines, Z. (2018, July 30). How can porn induce erectile dysfunction? Medical News Today. https://www.medicalnewstoday.com/articles/317117

Volkow, N. D., Koob, G. F., & McLellan, A. T. (2016). Neurobiologic advances from the brain disease model of addiction. *New England Journal of Medicine, 374*(4), 363-371. https://doi:10.1056/nejmra1511480

Voon, V., Mole, T. B., Banca, P., Porter, L., Morris, L., Mitchell... Irvine, M. (2014). Neural correlates of sexual cue reactivity in individuals with and without compulsive sexual behaviours. *PLoS ONE, 9*(7), e102419. https://doi.org/10.1371/journal.pone.0102419

Waisberg, J. L., & Porter, J. E. (1994). Purpose in life and outcome of treatment for alcohol dependence. *British Journal of Clinical Psychology, 33*(1), 49-63. https://doi.org/10.1111/j.2044-8260.1994.tb01093.x

Weinstein, A., Katz, L., Eberhardt, H., Cohen, K., & Lejoyeux, M. (2015). Sexual compulsion — Relationship with sex, attachment and sexual orientation. *Journal of Behavioural Addictions, 4*(1), 22-26. https://doi:10.1556/jba.4.2015.1.6

Weiss, D. (2013). *Clean: A proven plan for men committed to sexual integrity*. Thomas Nelson.

Weiss, D. (2020). What is intimacy anorexia? *Heart to Heart Counseling Center*. https://www.drdougweiss.com/what-is-intimacy-anorexia/

Weiss, R. (2004) *Treating sex addiction: A practical guide to diagnosis and treatment*. John Wiley and Sons.

## Reference list

Weiss, R. (2015, June 9). Gaslighting: How Addicts Drive Loved Ones Over the Edge. *PsychCentral.* https://blogs.psychcentral.com/sex/2014/05/gaslighting-how-addicts-drive-loved-ones-over-the-edge/

Wéry, A., & Billieux, J. (2017). Problematic cybersex: Conceptualization, assessment, and treatment. *Addictive Behaviours, 64,* 238-246. https://doi: 10.1016/j.addbeh.2015.11.007

Wilson, S., Strohsnitter, W., & Baecher-Lind, L. (2013). Practices and perceptions among pediatricians regarding adolescent contraception with emphasis on intrauterine contraception. *Journal of Pediatric and Adolescent Gynecology, 26*(5), 281-284. https://doi:10.1016/j.jpag.2013.05.004

Witkiewitz, K., Lustyk, M. K., & Bowen, S. (2013). Retraining the addicted brain: A review of hypothesized neurobiological mechanisms of mindfulness-based relapse prevention. *Psychology of Addictive Behaviors, 27*(2), 351-365. https://doi.org/10.1037/a0029258

Wright, P. J., Tokunaga, R. S., Kraus, A., & Klann, E. (2017). Pornography consumption and satisfaction: A meta-analysis. *Human Communication Research, 43*(3), 315-343. https://doi:10.1111/hcre.12108

Yoder, R. (2019, April 16). 5 tips for self-forgiveness in recovery. *Castle Craig Hospital.* https://castlecraig.co.uk/blog/2019/04/16/5-tips-for-self-forgiveness-in-recovery

Young, A. (2020). The Jekyll/Hyde of Sex Addiction: Compartmentalization. *Trailhead Counseling Center.* http://trailheadcounseling.com/the-jekyll-hyde-of-sex-addiction-compartmentalization/

Zweben, J. E., Yeary, J. EMDR in the treatment of addiction. (2013). In B. Carruth (Ed.), *Psychological Trauma and Addiction Treatment,* (pp. 129-142). Routledge. https://doi.org/10.4324/9781315808406

# Services and Offers

Sex addiction therapy for individuals and their partners, Gottman (level 1, 2), NLP, Hypnosis, NeurOptimal® neurofeedback, EMDR, trauma and PTSD management, infidelity recovery, Gestalt therapy, cognitive behavioural therapy, mindfulness practice, betrayal trauma, ADHD, depression and family therapy.

**Bonus for finishing this book:**
**30 minutes' free consultation with Dr Fai where you can have all your questions answered in private.**

**Contact details**
**Ph. 0413 482 486**
www.houseofhopecounsellingcentre.com.au
enquiries@houseofhopecounselling.com.au

# Notes

Notes

www.ingramcontent.com/pod-product-compliance
Lightning Source LLC
Chambersburg PA
CBHW071624080526
44588CB00010B/1256